The Religions
Next Door

Other Books by Marvin Olasky

On Fighting Poverty

*Compassionate Conservatism: What It Is, What It Does,
and How It Can Transform America*

*Renewing American Compassion: How Compassion
for the Needy Can Turn Ordinary Citizens into Heroes*

The Tragedy of American Compassion

Patterns of Corporate Philanthropy

More Than Kindness (with Susan Olasky)

On American History

*The American Leadership Tradition:
Moral Vision from Washington to Clinton*

*Fighting for Liberty and Virtue: Political and
Cultural Wars in Eighteenth-Century America*

*Philanthropically Correct: The Story of the Council
on Foundations*

Abortion Rites: A Social History of Abortion in America

Corporate Public Relations: A New Historical Perspective

On Journalism

Telling the Truth: How to Revitalize Christian Journalism

Central Ideas in the Development of American Journalism

The Press and Abortion, 1838–1988

*Prodigal Press: The Anti-Christian Bias of the
American News Media*

On Religion and Society

Standing for Christ in a Modern Babylon

Whirled Views (with Joel Belz)

Turning Point: A Christian Worldview Declaration
(with Herbert Schlossberg)

The Religions Next Door

What we need to know about **Judaism**, **Hinduism**, **Buddhism**, and **Islam**
—and what **reporters** are **missing**

Marvin Olasky

Broadman
& Holman
Publishers

NASHVILLE, TENNESSEE

0–8054–3143–8

Published by Broadman & Holman Publishers
Nashville, Tennessee

Dewey Decimal Classification: 291
Subject Heading: RELIGIONS
CHRISTIANITY AND OTHER RELIGIONS

Unless otherwise noted, Scripture quotations are from the Holy
Bible, New International Version, copyright
© 1973, 1978, 1984 by International Bible Society. Scripture
quotations marked NASB are from the New American Standard
Bible, © 1960, 1962, 1963, 1968, 1971, 1972, 1973, 1975, 1977;
used by permission. Quotations marked NKJV are from the
New King James Version, copyright © 1979, 1980, 1982,
Thomas Nelson, Inc., Publishers.

1 2 3 4 5 6 7 8 9 10   09 08 07 06 05 04

To Susan

Contents

Acknowledgments

Howard and Roberta Ahmanson, friends for over fifteen years, made it possible for me to write this book and to research Buddhism and Hinduism in Japan, India, and Cambodia. Samuel and Prema Sunder Raj and their children, Honda Yoshinari and his family, and David Willis were among those who showed hospitality on the other side of the world. University of Texas students who have taken my Journalism and Religion course over the past five years ran across many of the newspaper stories I quote in chapters 9 and 10, and asked searching questions.

Bits and pieces of many of the chapters have appeared in issues of *World*, ably led as always by publisher Joel Belz. The one human constant through all my adult life, through war and sadness, through boom and bust, for twenty-eight years of marriage, has been not baseball (although it's a strong contender) but my wife Susan. Even when I pray erratically, I thank God for her and for Pete, David, Daniel, and Benjamin, our four wonderful sons.

Introduction

James Sire's fine book *The Universe Next Door*, first published in 1976, was a response to a generation's run from religion. Many students brought up in mainline churches were finding preaching meaningless. It seemed that the demise of Christianity predicted by Clarence Darrow in 1925, after his big oratorical victory at Tennessee's "monkey trial," was not far off. Judging by the drift on university campuses, biblically faithful churches would soon be rare. Propelled by swirling winds, bright students were drifting toward faithless beliefs such as—to cite the subjects of three of Sire's chapters—naturalism, nihilism, and existentialism.

By the turn of the millennium, though, much had changed. Despite decades of mockery by media and academia leaders, Christianity was retaining some grip on 85 percent of Americans. For many that grip was tenuous, but with two generations educated largely from the perspective that God has nothing to do with history, literature, biology, or other subjects, surveys still showed an overwhelming majority of Americans believing that we owe our existence to God, not time plus chance. What's more, within Christianity adults were moving from Bible-doubting to Bible-believing churches in a wave so unmistakable that even the *New York Times* acknowledged in a headline, "Conservative Churches Grew Fastest in 1990's."

What about the young, the early twenty-first-century equivalent of the students Sire reached in the 1970s? Colleen Carroll's recent book *The New Faithful: Why Young Adults are Embracing Christian Orthodoxy* notes that many people in their twenties and thirties want to be able to profess a faith. Those who have grown up in homes broken by divorce and "a feeling of being saturated by greed, sex, and all the decadent forces in our culture" are harkening to churches where they don't have to say creeds with their fingers crossed. During two decades of teaching at the University of Texas, I've seen some of that among my own students.

Curiously, few journalists have written about the way Christianity has survived and even thrived. Imagine a person sentenced to death by numerous tribunals and then shot by a firing squad, hanged by the neck until dead, fried on an electric chair, poked with a lethal injection, and guillotined. What if after all that he was still alive and even able to pick up his head and reattach it to his neck? Wouldn't that be the story of the year? Yet the big story of Christian endurance in the last quarter of the twentieth century was right in front of thousands of American journalists, and virtually all missed it.

Reporters have also missed most of the international story. In the largest country geographically, the Soviet government spent most of the twentieth century teaching atheism to schoolchildren and persecuting adults who would not go along. Nevertheless, at century's end Christianity was roaring back in Russia and the Ukraine. In the biggest country by population, fifty years of force-feeding atheism to adults and children could not wipe out theistic yearnings. At the end of the century Christianity was stronger than ever in China, despite repeated government efforts to wipe it out.

Some bright students are concluding that the grass is greener in theological yards that once were far away but are now next door. Buddhism is attracting those turned on by the mythology of zen or the radiance of the Dalai Lama and his struggle against oppression. Hinduism has sunk deep roots since the time a generation ago when Hari Krishna devotees first danced along the Boston Common. Judaism, particularly in its Orthodox variety, is attracting some Jews who were highly secularized and others as well. As we will see, each of these religions generally receives more favorable press coverage than that offered concerning Christianity.

Islam also is growing, helped along by the surprisingly favorable treatment accorded it in the press and in schools. A recent report from the American Textbook Council entitled "Islam and the Textbooks" concluded that "on significant Islam-related subjects, textbooks omit, flatter, embellish and resort to happy talk, suspending criticism or harsh judgments that would raise provocative or even alarming questions." For example, the primary historical meaning of *jihad*—according to Bernard Lewis, the Princeton professor emeritus who is America's most distinguished scholar of Islam—has been the requirement "to bring the whole world under Islamic law." Yet the most-used world history text,

Prentice Hall's *Connections to Today*, merely tells students that *jihad* is an "effort in God's service" such as an "inner struggle to achieve spiritual peace."

The number of Hindus in America has increased during the past thirty years from 100,000 to almost a million. The number of Buddhists has similarly climbed, and perhaps five million Muslims now live in the United States, up from about 800,000 three decades ago; America may have almost as many Muslims as Jews. Religions that once were exotic in America are now next door, and pressures to clothe "the naked public square" will now come from not only conservative Christians but from others as well. We have come out of an era, unusual in the history of the world, where many intellectual leaders boasted of nakedness.

I grew up in that era and for a while dressed up in nakedness. At age thirteen I turned against my early instruction in Judaism and declared myself an atheist. For the next decade I remained one, before going through three years of transition that ended with my becoming a Christian at age twenty-six. Twenty-eight years later I remain one, but from my committed position I'm still interested in the paths others take. Some academics claim that an agnostic or atheist is best equipped to study religion because he will not be favorably inclined toward one or all of the beliefs he examines. And yet, just as my partial color blindness does not mean that I am objective about colors, so the lack of belief does not leave a person neutral about belief. Analysts who believe that the billions of people with some religious faith are pitifully deluded are not the best equipped to take faith seriously.

The pattern of this book is simple: I have tried to describe the practices of theologically conservative Judaism (chapter 1), Hinduism (chapter 3), Buddhism (chapter 5), and Islam (chapter 7) accurately and then show the various ways that I have personally encountered and evaluated them (chapters 2, 4, 6, and 8). The word *conservative* is important because each of these religions has (to make an analogy to constitutional interpretation) its strict constructionist and loose constructionist wings, made up of those who believe the scriptures of their religion must be followed closely, and those who take those scriptures as useful starting points but feel free to ignore or change instructions or practices that contradict typical beliefs and practices of modern society.

Chapters 1, 3, 5, and 7 emphasize the beliefs and practices of the "strict constructionists" for two reasons. First, contrary to what secularists expected, the conservative wings of these major religions are all growing faster than the liberal wings and increasingly asserting themselves. Second, the strict constructionists by their strictness stand against many modern trends and thus have belief and practice more distinctive than the loose constructionists who tend to go along and get along.

Chapters 2, 4, 6, and 8 vary according to the nature of the religions. Chapter 2 emphasizes history because that is crucial within Judaism. Chapter 4 examines the workings of the caste system, a crucial theological and social component of Hinduism. Chapter 6 looks at the way Buddhism has played out in today's most populous Buddhist country, Japan. Chapter 8 examines the connection of theology and politics within Islam in a world where terrorism and totalitarianism still create a regular diet of bad news.

The last two chapters then show what typical U.S. press accounts have made of this complexity, with many good and bad examples that University of Texas students and I have examined over the past few years. I want to thank the many students, from a variety of religious faiths, who have prodded my thinking. They have grown up in a land of choice, and sooner or later they will all have to choose.

Chapter One

Judaism's Rules

The worldwide Jewish population now numbers thirteen to eighteen million, with the largest concentrations in North America (perhaps 5.8 million) and Israel (about 4.7 million). Precision is difficult, though, because rabbis differ on who should be counted as Jewish and who should not. More Jews in the United States now marry non-Jews than Jews, and rabbis differ on whether the half-Jewish children of such couples should be counted as Jews; traditionally, only children born to a Jewish mother are considered Jewish.

Talking with a typical Jewish American today is largely the same as talking with his non-Jewish counterpart. Both are aware of Seinfeld and Madonna, bagels and KFC. Both are likely, if they feast at a religious table at all, to be shuffling through the cafeteria, choosing whatever spiritual dish suits their fancy at the moment. For many Jews the idea of moving from one religion to another is akin to moving from the Mickey Mouse Club to the Donald Duck Club: Why bother?

And yet the future may be with the minority of Jews who are strict constructionists in their understanding of the Bible. While only a decided minority of synagogue-going adults could be classified that way now, they are generally the ones having big families and sending their children to religious schools. The *Los Angeles Times,* in a recent report on twenty young men who were finishing a year of fourteen-hour-a-day Talmud study, quoted student David Cohen, "a serious man with intense dark eyes" who graduated from UCLA in 1999 after majoring in psychology. Cohen spoke of the psychology of his contemporaries: "They think they are having a fun time, but they are fooling themselves. They have a blast, and the next day they have a hangover. The kind of happiness you get from studying the Talmud doesn't leave you."

What is that happiness? Orthodox rabbis say it comes partly through knowledge gained and partly through the discipline of studying the Talmud, the volumes of biblical commentary put together during the four centuries after the destruction of the Temple in 70 AD. Rabbis talk of how the patience, persistence, and sometimes pugnacity in arguing a Talmudic point carry over into life generally. They in essence tell followers: Discipline your behavior, and your heart will eventually change; observe rituals before you know why, and understanding will come. The idea is that the rules, if followed, will so restrain our evil impulses that we will act in a decent way most of the time.

Traditional Judaism combines a high view of a man with a thorough list of commands designed to keep man from acting like a lowlife. Judaism gives high esteem to man, who did not evolve but was created in God's image as the crown of creation. As the Genesis account relates, God created man in a different way than he created animals, personally breathing into Adam the breath of life. Man can know God, worship him, and love him; animals cannot. Man—above the animals in rational ability, moral awareness, pursuit of beauty, use of language, and spiritual awareness—has dominion over them.

The Bible says that God gave people a perfect environment, the garden of Eden. God offered plenty of time for challenging intellectual work (studying animals, nature, and the world God created, and then naming things rightly) and pleasant physical breaks (tending a garden that produced great flowers and food, not thorns). We don't know what else God would have provided in the unlikely situation that Adam and Eve ran out of interesting things to do. But they sinned, and then—within Jewish teaching—it became vital to constrain sin by developing a detailed list of what to do and what not to do.

Jews say the rules are God made, and those who are orthodox cite chapter and verse of the Hebrew Scriptures (the Old Testament, in Christian parlance) to back up that contention. For example, look at some of the commands that touch on today's controversial questions involving sex. The Bible proscribes homosexuality, bestiality, and adultery (Lev. 18:22–23; Deut. 23:18). The Bible tells us not to engage in behavior that might put us on the path toward evil: for example, a man shall not wear women's clothing, and vice versa (Deut. 22:5). Since sin is always lurking at our door, we are not to indulge in familiarities with relatives, such as kissing or hugging, that might lead to incest (Lev. 18:6).

The Bible combines these precautions with counsel on how to build strong families by reverently fearing our fathers and mothers (Lev. 19:3), by being fruitful and multiplying (Gen. 1:28), and by refusing to sacrifice children (Lev. 18:21). But marriage is not only or even primarily for the purpose of having children: The first woman was created because "it is not good for man to be alone," so companionship and intimacy are vital functions of marriage. Husbands are not to withhold food, clothing, or conjugal rights from a wife (Exod. 21:10), and bridegrooms are to receive a year's exemption from taking part in any public labor, such as military service or guarding the wall (Deut. 24:5).

The list of commandments, both positive and negative, goes on: We are not to gossip, take revenge, leave sinners without rebuke, or stand by idly when a human life is in danger (Lev. 19:16–18). We are to keep our word (Deut. 23:21) and not swear needlessly (Exod. 20:7). We are not to give occasion to the simple-minded to stumble on the road (Lev. 19:14), and we are not eat or drink like gluttons or drunkards (Lev. 19:26; Deut. 21:20). We are not to testify falsely (Exod. 20:13).

The commandments include ones concerning economics: not to do wrong in buying or selling (Lev. 25:14), not to borrow on interest (Deut. 23:20, because this would cause the lender to sin), not to defraud (Lev. 19:13) or commit fraud in measuring (Lev. 19:35). Many rules concern employer-employee relations, such as the importance of paying a hired man his wages (Lev. 19:13). Many commandments concern property rights: we are not to deny falsely another's property rights (Lev. 19:11), remove boundary markers (Deut. 19:14), or destroy fruit trees wantonly or even in warfare (Deut. 20:19–20).

Biblical contracts always cut two ways: the hired laborer shall be permitted to eat of the produce he reaps, but he shall not take more than he can eat (Deut. 23:25–26). Those under a manager's authority also have rights: servants must be dealt with in accordance with the laws pertaining to them (Exod. 21:2–6), and we are not to muzzle even a beast while it is working in produce that it could eat and enjoy (Deut. 25:4).

Numerous commandments outline duties to the poor: for example, we are not to demand from a poor man repayment of his debt when the creditor knows that he cannot pay (Exod. 22:25). We are also not to take in pledge against debts utensils used in preparing food (Deut. 24:6), and we are not to take a pledge from a widow (Deut. 24:17). We are to give charity (Deut. 15:11) and refrain from hurting widows or orphans (Exod. 22:21). We are to leave for gleaning by the poor the unreaped corners of a field or orchard, the imperfect clusters in a vineyard, and the grapes that have fallen to the ground (Lev. 19:9–10). We are not to treat a Hebrew servant harshly (Lev. 25:43), and we are to give him good gifts when he finishes his term of service (Deut. 15:14).

Commands are for the mighty as well as the lowly: a judge, for example, needs to be well versed in Torah law (Deut. 1:17) and careful to treat parties in a litigation with impartiality (Lev. 19:15). He is not to favor a rich or powerful man when trying a case (Lev. 19:15), but he is also not to be affected by the poverty of one of the parties

(Exod. 23:3; Lev. 19:15). He is not to take a bribe or to render a decision on the basis of personal opinion but only on the evidence of two witnesses who saw what actually occurred (Exod. 23:7–8).

On and on it goes: traditional Judaism produces the guarded life. Why must those commands be followed? Because they come from God who made everything in the universe: "In the beginning God created the heavens and the earth. The earth was formless and void, and darkness was over the surface of the deep. . . . Then God said, 'Let there be light'; and there was light" (Gen. 1:1, 3 NASB). If the commands did not come from God, they could be followed or discarded based on individual preference, so strict constructionist Jews spend a lot of time showing that the five books of Moses and succeeding parts of Scripture actually came from God.

Strict constructionist Jews defend intensely the accuracy of the Hebrew Scriptures. The "broken windows" theory of crime prevention—sweat the small things because cities that allow minor property destruction soon see their rape and murder statistics rising—works in assessing scriptural credibility as well. Since the Bible throughout claims that it is God's communication with man, factual inaccuracies, uncovered through the work of archeologists, could torpedo that claim. Material that's accurate in its specific detail attests to the reliability of the whole.

For that reason strict constructionists have rejoiced as accounts from Genesis considered mythical by some nineteenth-century scholars have gained new archeological support. For example, famous German scholar Julius Wellhausen considered the Genesis story of Abraham rescuing Lot "simply impossible," but archeological research now shows the details of that story to have been accurate. The conventional wisdom was that the city of Ur from which Abraham supposedly came did not exist, but excavations now show Ur to have been an advanced city. For a long time some archeologists viewed the Sodom and Gomorrah story as fiction, but excavations at Tell Mardikh uncovered tablets mentioning both those cities as having been destroyed.

Moving further into the Bible: the nineteenth-century view was that Moses would probably have been illiterate, so someone else must have written the five books ascribed to him, but historians now recognize that the Egyptian upper class was highly literate. Scholars at one point said that the Hittites described in the Bible did not exist, nor did rulers such as Belshazzar of Babylon or Sargon of Assyria. Archeologists now have records of all those civilizations and reigns.

The Old Testament refers by name to about forty kings during the sixteen hundred-year period from 2000 to 400 BC. If those names were inaccurate or out of order, that would also be a strike against biblical reliability. But Princeton's Robert Wilson, who knew twenty-six ancient languages and dialects and so could read just about all that remains from the ancient Near East, came to a different conclusion. He wrote, in *A Scientific Investigation of the Old Testament,* that "no stronger evidence for the substantial evidence of the Old Testament record could possibly be imagined than the collection of kings. Mathematically, it is one chance in [750 with 21 zeroes after it] that this accuracy is mere circumstance."

We could examine many more proofs of biblical integrity, but all point to strong scriptural defensibility on the grounds of factual accuracy. And yet here's another argument put forward by critics: why couldn't editors and copyists have kept the factual framework and distorted the doctrines to conform to their own prejudices? After all, we do not have the original scrolls; they are long gone. No one tried to preserve scrolls hundreds of years old, and there was no way to do so except in terrible desert conditions since moisture is the enemy of parchment. (Look at the climate control we need to preserve the relatively recent Declaration of Independence.) Old copies were burned or buried. For a long time the earliest existing manuscript of the Old Testament that we still have, called the Masoretic Text, was dated around 900 AD.

That argument had some potential, but in 1947 people found two thousand-year-old scrolls hidden in a desert cave near Israel's Dead Sea. The Dead Sea scrolls contained portions from the book of Isaiah and other Bible books that are virtually identical to the ones we have now. That means the copying over the years was accurate; only a few verses are questionable, usually because of small variations in words and spelling that do not throw any doctrines into question. As the historian Flavius Josephus wrote about the Hebrew Scriptures even in the first century AD, "although long ages have now passed, no one has ventured even to add, or to remove, or to alter a syllable."

Besides, copying records show how hard scribes worked to transmit accurately what they received. Old Testament copyists from 100 to 500 AD wrote exactly thirty letters on each line of parchment, and every letter had to be written while the scribe referred to the original manuscript; writing from memory was banned. For easy checking each book ended on a prescribed line on the parchment and was checked and rechecked. Frederic Kenyon, the British Museum's director and principal librarian, put it this way: "The same extreme care which was devoted to the transcription of manuscripts is also at the bottom of the disappearance of the earlier copies. When a manuscript had been copied with the exactitude prescribed by the Talmud, and had been duly verified, it was accepted as authentic and regarded as being of equal value with any other copy. If all were equally correct, age gave no advantage to a manuscript."

Here's one more possibility: What if the original writing and down-the-centuries copying were accurate, but the biblical history was pious propaganda, stories made up by writers to create devotees? Here it's important to see that beyond accuracy stands realism: The Bible is different from other scriptures that treat religious founders and ancestors as demigods. Biblical writers, rather than exalting their ancestors, often portrayed giants as ethical pygmies. Noah, recently saved from death by flood, got passed-out drunk. Abraham, fearing for his life, may have been ready to pimp his wife. Jacob was a deceiver; Samson, a muscular twit; David, an adulterer who covered up that act by having a loyal captain killed. If the Bible's goal was propaganda, its writers were incompetent, and yet that's not what readers moved by surpassing beauty tend to infer.

In essence Judaism makes a strong case for those who believe in God to become believers in Judaism. If there is a God who created the world and created man in his own image, we know that God communicates since we communicate. Since we speak and write, he would speak and write; and unless he is cruel, it is likely that he would give us information and perspective that would help us to live well in the world in which he has placed us. Orthodox Jews thus say that when we are holding a copy of the Hebrew Scriptures in our hands, it is likely that we are holding a message from God; and since he is wiser than us, we should not place our thoughts above his.

Until AD 70, Jews were to show their faith in God by following his rules, but they did have a safety net, the sacrificial system. Ritual slaughters at the temple must sometimes have been wading in blood, as those aware that they had broken the rules tried to make themselves right with God by sacrificing cattle, sheep, doves, and other animals. When Roman armies destroyed the temple, they also eliminated the safety net. Jews realized that since their eternal lives depended on observing the rules, they had better not even come close to breaking them; and the way to do that was to set up a second set of rules far beyond the biblical set.

The massive record of rabbinical debates known as the Talmud shows how that second set of rules came into being. Few non-Jews understand the importance of the Talmud. Scholar Jacob Neusner writes, "Nearly all Christians view

Judaism not as a religion in its own terms, but merely as Christianity without Christ, pretty much the same religion but deeply flawed by the rejection of you know who. . . . Few grasp that Judaism is not merely 'not-Christianity' or that Judaism reads the written Torah in light of the Torah of Sinai, orally formulated and orally transmitted."

The Talmud was said to be that "oral Torah," the record of laws, observances, applications, and understandings given by God orally to Moses and passed from one generation of sages to the next. Saying they were merely going by the oral Torah, the Talmudic rabbis created a new safety net by regulating almost every aspect of behavior throughout the week.

For example, where Exodus 23:19 stated, "Do not cook a young goat in its mother's milk," the Talmud made sure that goats would not be cooked in any milk, and teeth that tasted goat would not taste milk at the same meal. Talmudic rabbis morphed the Exodus injunction into rules that meat of any kind and dairy products of any kind could never be eaten together or within a period of several hours. Dishes or utensils that came into contact with one class of food could never be used with another.

The written Bible stipulates that God rested from his work on the Sabbath and his followers should do so also. Talmudic rabbis saw *melakhah*—the word often translated as *work*—as any "activity that influences the physical world." They laid out thirty-nine categories of forbidden activity (including sowing, plowing, reaping, grinding, kneading, baking, shearing wool, or spinning) and, to preclude any transgression, defined those activities expansively. Forbidden activities included weaving or separating two threads or more; tying, untying, or sewing two stitches or more; tearing, writing, or erasing two or more letters; kindling a fire; or carrying any object outside of the home.

To this day Orthodox Jews do not light a fire of any kind on the Sabbath. Since driving a car requires putting a key into the ignition, which produces a spark, driving is prohibited. Pets also should not work on the Sabbath, so pet owners should not have their dogs retrieve newspapers for them on that day. Any use of electricity—turning on a light or a stove, opening a refrigerator—is also forbidden. Orthodox synagogues have traditionally hired a non-Jew, a "shabbat goy," to turn on and off lights or furnaces; a young Colin Powell earned some money in that category.

Today rabbis continue to apply Talmudic insights to explain exactly what is and is not proper. For example, Leviticus 19:19 and Deuteronomy 22:9–11 prohibit the mingling of different kinds of substances, including mixing wool and linen in the same piece of clothing; that is called *shaatnez*. Rabbis have interpreted this to disallow a wool suit with linen-threaded buttons but to allow a linen tie worn with a wool suit. Shoulder pads in suits and embroidery on sweaters may be trouble. Orthodox Jews are to take suits to be tested in a *shaatnez* lab; cities with Orthodox communities often have one.

Behind what some see as trivia is a great theological problem. Put simply, it was and is this: up to the destruction of the temple in AD 70, Israelites could not be saved by keeping the law, for even the greatest often transgressed it. They needed the sacrifice of atonement made in the temple, for without the shedding of blood there was no remission of sin. The sin could be transferred to an innocent animal, a scapegoat, that was then slaughtered in the temple as payment for transgression. But the sacrifices stopped when the temple was destroyed. With all the precautions the Talmudists took, it was still likely that everyone at some time would break some of God's laws. How, then, could people be saved?

Some rabbis pointed out that the situation was particularly perilous because God's law might proscribe not only actions but states of mind. What if the sixth commandment prohibits not only murder but murderous thoughts or the seventh commandment forbids not only adultery but sexual fantasizing? And if someone somehow was in such total control of his thoughts throughout his life that he did not fall into one of those ravines, what about the final commandment's prohibition of coveting? Was anyone totally immune from that?

Christians have an answer to that problem: Christ's sacrifice is the good-for-all-time safety net that animal sacrifices once were. The Talmud gave another answer: set up the barriers well away from the real barriers so that commands were less likely to be broken. But some rabbis have suggested a third: God is a lenient God, and as long as a person's good deeds, prayer, and study outweigh his failings, that is good enough. Interestingly, some have also said: Wait for the messiah.

The great medieval Jewish theologian Rabbi Moshe ben Maimon (also known as "Maimonides" or "Rambam") developed a list of thirteen principles of faith that he said were the minimal requirements for Jewish belief. Over the centuries they have been widely accepted, and can be compared to the Nicene Creed in Christianity or to the Five Pillars of Islam. The first five emphasize that God exists; that he is one and unique, body-less, and eternal; and that prayer is to be directed to God alone and to no one else.

The fifth through ninth of Maimonides thirteen principles of faith deal with God's communication to us. The principles state that the words of the prophets are true; Moses was the greatest of the prophets; God gave Moses the written Torah (the first five books of the Bible) and the Oral Torah (the Talmud). The last four of Maimonides thirteen principles deal with judgment and what happens at the end: God knows the thoughts and deeds of men, God will reward the good and punish the wicked, the Messiah will come, and the dead will be resurrected. Maimonides twelfth principle is, "I believe with perfect faith in the coming of the messiah, and though he may tarry, still I await him every day."

So in Judaism, as in Christianity, the coming of the messiah is crucial; but since the concept is different, it may be clearer to use the Hebrew word *moshiach* (pronounced moh-SHEE-ak) when referring to the Jewish messiah. The *moshiach* is not a savior, is not divine, and does not sacrifice himself to pay for the sins of others. The *moshiach* is a great governmental and military leader who is also learned and wise. Most leading rabbis believe that the time of the *moshiach's* return depends on the conduct of mankind. Some say he will come when things are getting worse (to save the day) and some when things are getting better (as a reward). Orthodox Jews believe that the prophet Elijah, taken to heaven alive, will return to announce the *moshiach's* imminent appearance.

When the *moshiach* comes, Jews will return to Israel, wickedness will decrease, Jerusalem will be rebuilt, religious courts of justice reestablished, and a descendant of King David enthroned. Jerusalem will be the center of all world government, all nations will be at peace with one another, and Judaism will be recognized universally as the one true religion. Temple worship will be restored with new thanksgiving sacrifices but without sin offerings, which will not be needed because sin will have vanished. Elijah will answer all questions about doctrine and will show who has the right ancestry to be the high priest in resumed temple worship.

Maimonides wrote that in this messianic age men will not be immortal or transported to paradise. Instead it will be a period when Jews live in Israel under a great king whose name is known throughout the world, with many nations subject to him and living in peace. It will be easier for people to earn their daily bread, but rich and poor will still exist. Still humanity will be freed from war, and people will be able to study philosophy and God's laws. The *moshiach* eventually will die, and his son will succeed him as Israel's king. "We hope for the messiah not because we will enjoy great prosperity, ride on horses, drink wine, and enjoy fine music," Maimonides wrote, but so as to "benefit from his wisdom and closeness to God."

However, a sage of the following century, Rabbi Moshe ben Nachman (also known as Ramban or Nachmanides) said that when the *moshiach* comes nature will radically change and the earth will be like the garden of Eden, with wild animals tame, and people once again having all the potential that Adam and Eve had before they sinned. In recent years some Zionists have thought that the creation of Israel as an independent country showed the importance of human effort; others have suggested that the United Nations will bring about what Maimonides hoped for. So there has been no consensus within Judaism, except one: Jesus of Nazareth was not the messiah.

Judaism also differs from Christianity by lacking the concept of the Holy Spirit, the third person of the Trinity who is said to help people by grace to live as befits a follower of God. In the absence of such grace, the rules are essential. Christians read the fifth chapter of the Gospel of John and are astounded that when Jesus healed on the Sabbath a man who had been paralyzed for thirty-eight years, the Pharisees did not rejoice that the man could now walk but were angry at Jesus for violating the rules. Orthodox Jews say "of course" to the strict application of the rules in that instance because if we ignore the rules, we have no firm ground on which to stand. The Talmud is both ground and map.

Today many American Jews are nonobservant: they are often proud of Jewish ethnicity but do not engage in synagogue worship and may not believe in God. Those who do participate at times in synagogue worship fall into six camps. Two, the Orthodox and the Hasidic, try to live by the Bible and the Talmud. Two others, Reform and Reconstructionist, pay no attention to the Talmud and see the Bible as a collection of nonbinding but worth-reading narratives. A fifth group, Conservative Judaism, searches for a middle road. A sixth group, Messianic Jews, rejects the Talmud and believes that Jesus was the promised Messiah.

Reform Jews are the largest of these groups. They believe in one God who can be worshipped in ways that individual Jews choose, since Jewish law is changeable. For example, the creation saga of Genesis should be understood symbolically, with Satan as a symbol of selfish desires. Most Reform Jews believe that God forgives all, and if there is an afterlife, it will best be grasped by those who have been kind to their neighbors, for whatever reason. The emphasis is on leading an ethical life, with good ethics defined by major contemporary philosophers.

Reform Jews believe that God may have inspired the Torah—the five books of Moses—but it is still a document of its time that must be reinterpreted for our time; laws given then are not binding now. Abortion, for example, is not a step to be taken casually, but the decision is a personal one for the mother to take, preferably during the first forty days of pregnancy. Homosexuality is also a lifestyle choice not to be criticized. Reconstructionist Jews (only 1 percent, but with a strong intellectual following) take similar positions on social issues. They generally consider Sinai to be mythical or irrelevant but favor the maintenance of the culture that grew out of belief that Sinai was real.

Orthodox and Hasidic groups took a body blow when Hitler destroyed their central European havens, but they are making a comeback fueled in part by demographics: Orthodox and Hasidic Jews tend to have large families, Reform and nonobservant Jews very small ones. Orthodox Jews believe that every word of the Hebrew Scriptures is inspired by God and try to follow Talmudic instruction in every respect; Hasidic Jews are similar but give more of a role to individual inspiration and tend to have exuberant worship.

Conservative Jews attempt to find a middle-of-the-road position between the Orthodox and Reform varieties. Conservative Jews believe that the Torah was not communicated to Moses but was written much later in response to God's revelation of himself at Mount Sinai. Messianic Jews are not counted as such by many Jews: they maintain synagogue-style worship and try to follow most of the 613 commandments but also believe that Jesus is the Messiah and was foretold throughout the Old Testament. Messianic Jews—the best-known group is Jews for Jesus—are strict constructionists who walk to a different exegesis. Their conservative social practices and political leanings are often similar to those among the Orthodox and Hasidic.

Holidays unite these strands. The major holidays for American Jews today are Rosh Hashanah, Yom Kippur, Sukkot (a traditional harvest festival), Hanukah, Purim, Passover, Shavuot (the day Moses is said to have given the Ten Commandments), and Tish'a B'Av. They all run from sundown to sundown, since Jewish days start in the evening.

Rosh Hashanah, in the early fall, is New Year's Day, celebrating the creation of the world. On *Yom Kippur,* the day of atonement, the ritual of Kaparot includes a person swinging a chicken over his head while chanting a prayer for atonement; the chicken is then slaughtered and given to the poor. The twirling and killing signifies that this should happen to the person as well, unless God is merciful. Adults fast throughout the day and also refrain from sex, bathing, and wearing leather shoes. At the close of Yom Kippur, when a shofar, ram's horn, is blown, the future is sealed.

Hanukkah, an eight-day festival usually celebrated in December, is a minor holiday that has become major in recent decades so that Jewish children don't feel left out as neighbors celebrate Christmas. Hanukkah celebrates the victory of Jewish fundamentalists, the Maccabees, over a remnant of Alexander the Great's empire in 165 BC. The Greo-Syrians in charge of Palestine thumbed their noses at Judaism by sacrificing pigs on the temple altar, and a revolt began. Its triumph was marked by a rededication of the temple, and that required having a menorah (lamp) that would keep burning day after day. Although the lamp had only a one-day supply of oil, it miraculously burned for eight days, which was enough time to get a fresh supply of oil.

Purim is a festive holiday near the end of winter that commemorates the narrow Jewish escape from destruction recorded in the book of Esther. Haman, an early Hitler in ancient Persia, wanted to kill all the Jews, but a providential ordering of events led to his death and Jewish triumph. The holiday is traditionally known for adult drinking and children's consumption of pastries.

Passover is an eight-day spring holiday that celebrates Israelite liberation from Egyptian slavery, as related in the book of Exodus. The holiday is marked by *seders*—ceremonial dinners—and the exclusion of bread or anything that contains leaven from the household. Blood from a sacrificed lamb, placed on the doorpost of Jewish homes, made the angel of death pass over Jewish homes and kill the firstborn sons of Egyptians. Near the close of the seder, celebrants pray for the *moshiach* to come soon.

One of Passover's significant customs involves the removal of *chametz* (leaven) from Jewish homes; this commemorates the need to escape so quickly from Egypt that they did not have time to let their bread rise. The practice also symbolizes removal of "puffiness," pride, from our lives. Orthodox Jews scour their homes to remove any trace of leaven, even to the extent of going over the edges of stoves and refrigerators with toothpicks and Q-Tips. Pockets and vacuum cleaner bags must be emptied.

Any leavened food that contains wheat, barley, oats, rye, or spelt, and any dishes used with such food, must be disposed of or locked up in a *chametz* closet. Orthodox Jews who own pets or cattle must even change their diets during Pesach. Since it is prohibited even to own any *chametz* during Pesach, or utensils used in cooking anything with *chametz*, Orthodox Jews will "sell" what they have to a non-Jew for an eight-day period; pets and cattle who will be eating *chametz* may also be "sold." Animals and objects do not have to be physically removed as long as they are under the ownership of someone else.

Tisha B'Av (the ninth day of the month of Av) is the saddest day in Judaism, a twenty-four-hour fast commemorating the days (in 586 BC and AD 70) on which both the first and second temples were destroyed. On this date also, in AD 1290 and 1492, the rulers of England and Spain expelled Jews; in AD 135 and 1914, the revolt of would-be messiah Bar Kochba failed, and World War I began.

Judaism Glossary

Ashkenazic Jews Those who lived primarily in northern Europe—primarily Germany, Poland, and Russia.

Bar Mitzvah A rite of passage for a thirteen-year-old boy, who reads the Torah publicly and then often has an expensive party; he is then considered a man for purposes of community worship. Reform and Conservative Jews now celebrate Bat Mitzvahs for girls.

Circumcision Removal of the foreskin of a penis, done by a ritual surgeon called a *mohel* eight days after birth.

Cohen Hebrew word for a descendant of Aaron capable of conducting priestly, sacrificial worship at the temple.

Diaspora The collective name for all countries outside of Israel; where most Jews have lived since at least AD 70.

Ghetto Special district in cities to which Jews in medieval times were often confined.

Halakhah Rules, largely based on the Talmud, that govern the life of Orthodox and Hasidic Jews as to when to pray, how to eat, etc.

Hasidism Largely orthodox Jews who also have mystical beliefs derived from the Kabbalah. The Lubavitch (Chabad) movement is the best-known Hasidic grouping in the U.S.

Hebrew Scriptures What Christians call the Old Testament: Torah, prophets, and writings.

Israelites Term describing ancient Jews, as compared to Israelis, which refers to the Jews of modern Israel.

Kaddish A traditional prayer, recited at the end of a synagogue worship service and also in memory of the dead, that praises God's holiness.

Kashrut Jewish dietary rules which tell how to keep kosher by not eating proscribed foods and by strenuously working to keep meat and dairy products apart.

Levite In ancient Israel a member of the Israelite tribe that provided temple helpers, musicians, and teachers.

Mezuzah A small box, affixed to the doorpost of homes, that contains a piece of paper with the words of the shema in Hebrew written on it. Orthodox and Hasidic Jews touch the mezuzah and say a blessing when they enter and leave home.

Minyan Ten men, the minimum for public prayer.

Mohel The ritual surgeon who performs circumcisions.

Oral Torah Talmudic rabbis said this was passed down from Moses to disciples through the centuries and finally incorporated into the Talmud. Rabbis contended that God gave the written Torah at Mt. Sinai but the oral Torah as well.

Parve Food that is neither milk nor meat (vegetables, bread, fruit) and can be eaten in a meal with either.

Rabbi "My teacher" (in Hebrew), an expert in religious law who leads worship and counsels synagogue members.

Rebbe The main leader of a Hasidic community.

Sephardic Jews Jews whose ancestors lived in Spain and north Africa.

Shema Confession of faith from Deuteronomy 6:4: "Hear O Israel, the Lord our God, the Lord is One. And you shall love the Lord your God with all your heart, with all your soul and with all your might." A slip of paper with these words is placed within a mezuzah and also recited during fixed daily prayers.

Shoah Hebrew word for the Holocaust, the killing of six millions Jews by Nazis during World War II.

Synagogue The main place of worship for Jews since the destruction of the temple in AD 70.

TaNaK Acronym formed from the Hebrew words Torah (five books of Moses), Neviim ("Prophets" from Joshua through Jeremiah), and Ketuvim ("Writings" such as Psalms, Proverbs, etc.).

Torah The first five books of the Bible: Genesis, Exodus, Leviticus, Numbers, and Deuteronomy.

Yiddish A dialect of German written in Hebrew characters that was used in Germany and Poland from the late medieval period through modern times.

Chapter Two

Hermits in a
Shopping Mall

When I ask my students to word-associate concerning Judaism, most non-Jews come up blank. "A guy wears a thingy on his head," one wrote. When I do the same, many memories flood back, most of them good: walking to the synagogue as a child with my father on Saturdays. Lighting the menorah on Hanukah and receiving presents. Fasting increasing amounts of time on Yom Kippur, the Day of Atonement, until at age twelve I fasted the entire day—only to give up the practice entirely two years later. But above all, year after year, learning the history: why Jews are the chosen people (chosen mostly for trouble, it seemed). How Jews faced persecution, largely from Christians, over the centuries.

What I learned, and what the Bible does teach, is that God's commands to the Israelites to be holy meant that they were to separate themselves from the unholy cultures that surrounded them in Canaan. The Hebrew Scriptures also record God's giving to the Israelites a narrow land of milk and honey distinct from the desert areas to the east. But separation from other cultures was difficult, particularly in Canaan.

God could have given the Israelites some out-of-the-way venue. Instead he placed them on a strip of ground that forms the land bridge between Asia/Europe and Africa. Egyptians, Babylonians, or Macedonians out to conquer the ancient world marched through a land that was sometimes a battlefield and always a place where cultures clashed and new ideas came into play.

Either God made a mistake equivalent to dropping a person into a shopping mall and commanding him to be a hermit, or he was forcing the Israelites, like it or not, to become a transforming influence on other cultures. Which was it? Forcing people to do what they otherwise would avoid is one of God's clear patterns of behavior; the book of Jonah shows this process. A William Ewer-Cecil Browne jingle about Christian anti-Semitism (often attributed to Hilaire Belloc and others) goes, "How odd of God / To choose the Jews, / But not so odd / As those who choose / the Jewish God / And spurn the Jews." A parallel ditty about Israel's location could go, "How odd that God / said 'Be apart' / Yet placed His people / at their start / in the world's ancient / merchandise mart."

Actually, there's no mistake, and nothing odd about it, at least from a Christian perspective. Christians believe that Old Testament commands never to sin cannot be met by sinful man, so they bring us face-to-face with the need for forgiveness through Christ. Old Testament commands to separate also could not be met, so they pushed some Israelites to see that they had no choice but to be a light to the Gentiles, transforming those cultures in order to stay alive themselves.

The descendants of Abraham, Isaac, and Jacob, almost always living among other peoples and confronting other cultures, helped to convert some of their neighbors. When they left Egypt, a mixed multitude of non-Israelites went with them. When they settled in Canaan amid many other nations, they intermarried and brought into Israel people like Ruth, the great-grandmother of King David.

Meanwhile Israelites tried to hack out of the jungle of faiths that surrounded them, a holiness theme park in which everything—laws, customs, food, clothing—would point to God's holiness. Not helped by their location, they failed. And when the giant grindstones of Assyria and Babylonia came up against Israel's stone tablets, sparks flew. A third choice appeared: separation, transformation, or appeasement. The captives in Assyria became appeasers, giving up what faith in God remained among them in order to become an ordinary part of the imperial population.

Though captives in Babylonia, Daniel, Shadrach, Meshach, and Abednego, became transformers, studying Babylonian culture and then influencing kings Nebuchadnezzar and Cyrus to believe in God. Transformers always had to fight a two-front war. They had to battle appeasers who could give up faith in God in return for easy acceptance by the idol worshippers around them. They also had to struggle with separatists who would hold tightly to the light God had given them but hide it under a basket for fear that others would see it and snuff it out.

The battle within Israel of those three groups raged for centuries. The first major political upheaval of the post-Old

Testament era began in 333 BC when Alexander the Great swept through West Asia and conquered many nations, including Israel. Some Israelites separated from Greek-influenced society and formed a community near the Dead Sea at Qumran. (Two thousand years later their records were found and called "the Dead Sea Scrolls.") Others became Hellenistic appeasers, aping the Greeks. A third group emphasized transformation, sometimes through military means.

Roman rule came in 63 BC, and not peaceably: Roman legions under Pompey killed thousands, including temple priests at the altar. And yet, because those who follow biblical rules tend to honor marriage, work hard, and build big families, by around 4 BC Jews made up about 10 percent of the Roman Empire. That's about the time when a Jewish baby named Yeshua, born in a stable, became one of approximately 8 million Jews then in the world, with 2.5 million living in their ancient homeland (according to the *Encyclopaedia Judaica*).

Almost all of them had to interact with Roman culture, and many attempted to transform it not by warfare but by proselytizing. Some thought the two means of transformation could go together, with Jews, under the leadership of a Messiah, becoming the dominant influence in the Roman Empire. Leaders periodically claimed messianic status, and Palestine became such a hard place to rule that in AD 26 Rome gave the Jerusalem command to hard-edged Pontius Pilate. He tried to quash all opposition by crucifying during the next decade over ten thousand Jews, including that Yeshua, called Jesus in Greek.

Yeshua's small band of followers soon put out the unnatural claim that their leader was resurrected from the dead. Astoundingly, over the next two decades thousands of Jews believed that. One former Pharisee who came to believe that, Paul, became a major-league transformer as he traveled throughout the Empire to explain to non-Jewish audiences that Jesus is the Son of God. As new Christians learned biblical patterns of thought, they transformed every aspect of their lives.

But in what had been the Holy Land itself, most Jews did not believe in Christ. Zealots inspired them to believe that if they battled Rome militarily God would come to their aid. When one failed rebellion led to the demolition of the temple in AD 70, an estimated 100,000 Jews died, with another 100,000 taken to Rome as slaves and more fleeing to other countries. Three years later a Roman army surrounded the last Jewish force, which had dug in at Masada, a mountain fortress. All the defenders committed suicide.

Believers in Christ and those still waiting for a *moshiach* then competed to explain to Jews and others what needed to be done now that the center of Jewish worship, the temple, no longer existed. Those with faith in Jesus did better at this, for Jesus had predicted the temple's destruction, and apostles were already explaining how each believer was a temple for the Holy Spirit. As Donald Akenson notes in *Surpassing Wonder,* "The Jesus-faith was much quicker to [develop] a temple-religion-without-a-temple than were the founders of what became known as the Jewish faith. . . . The Christian construct is older than the Jewish one."

After Christianity and Judaism clearly split between AD 80 and 100, the two religions competed for proselytes over the next two centuries. (The word *proselyte* itself initially referred to converts to Judaism.) The competition became increasingly bitter, with both sides at times acting like warring brothers bringing troublemaking tales about the other to Roman authorities. Words sometimes turned into sticks and stones, leaving a bitterness that turned back into words about the violence each side purportedly visited upon the other.

Judaism initially was on top, but in Judea and elsewhere Messiah-less Jews went to war under the banner of those who claimed to be God's anointed leader. Jewish rebels in AD 115 and 116 in Cyrene and Egypt destroyed pagan temples and the tomb of Pompey, the Roman general who had captured Jerusalem in 63 BC. Counterattacking Roman legions then killed thousands of Jews, and those who survived saw their property confiscated so that the destroyed temples could be restored.

The last great rebellion began in AD 132 when Rome's Emperor Hadrian banned circumcision and decided to rebuild Jerusalem as a pagan city. Troops led by Simeon bar Kochba—certified as the Messiah by the revered Rabbi Akiva—were initially successful. But new Roman soldiers arrived and killed (often in exceptionally cruel ways) bar Kochba, Akiva, and several hundred thousand others, with that many again sold as slaves. Rome gave Jerusalem the name Aelia Capitolina and prohibited Jews from living there.

Meanwhile Christians proceeded in a slow, one-by-one conversion process, and they gradually succeeded in transforming the Roman Empire. Where Christianity gained influence, children—unwanted by their fathers and left outside to die—gained a new opportunity to live. Poor people who had settled for bread and circuses went to work and built families. Slaves received better treatment and sometimes liberation. Women also treated as property realized that God knew them by name, and Paul recorded the names of some in his epistles.

The different strategies of Christianity and Judaism contributed to different results. By the fourth century Christianity was winning, and it gained a big breakthrough with the dramatic conversion of Roman Emperor Constantine to Christianity in AD 312. The Edict of Milan in 313 granted toleration to all religions, including Christianity and Judaism, but only ten years after that edict a sad tendency emerged: some Christian leaders began using their new governmental power to give their position the advantage. In 325 the Council of Nicea, along with formulating the terms of the classic Nicene Creed, restricted the political and religious rights of Jews. In 337 legislation in the eastern half of the Empire forbade Jews from owning slaves, Christians and Jews from intermarrying, and women from converting to Judaism.

During the following centuries some localities went further. Alexandria, Egypt, expelled Jews in 411, and Minorca, Spain, in 418 gave its Jewish inhabitants a choice of "conversion" or expulsion. (Conversion is in quotation marks because true conversion is based on belief, not any specific actions, and belief cannot be forced; the Roman Catholic Church, however, came to believe that baptism was efficacious regardless of belief.) In 576 and 582 the Franks, who

controlled much of what is now France, and in 613 the
Visigoths, who ruled much of what is now Spain, also
ordered Jews within their territories to "convert" or leave.

Jews responded predictably in 712 by helping Muslim
invaders conquer Spain. In other parts of Europe, restrictive
legislation arose over the next several centuries, with Jewish
families pushed from place to place and often leading lives
that anticipated the last three of Thomas Hobbes's famous
adjectives: nasty, brutish, and short. But those lives did not
fit the first two adjectives, solitary and poor, because communities—including ones newly planted in France—often
developed strong bonds. Jews worked at whatever urban
trades were allowed to them, and a few usually became moneylenders, since the church did not allow Christians to compete with them.

Those moneylenders sometimes became rich. Jewish economic success led to jealousy and covetousness among the
nominally Christian, who sought opportunities to steal.
The great opportunity arose after Pope Urban II in 1095
called for a crusade to retake Jerusalem. As participants in the
First Crusade headed toward Palestine, some killed along
the way up to ten thousand Jews from communities in
northern France and along the Rhine (about one-fourth to
one-third of the Jewish population of the area). Other crusades brought similar destruction, and popes sometimes
offered, as an incentive for Crusade participation, the cancel-
lation of Crusaders' debts to Jews.

Roman Catholic doctrinal changes also contributed to
increased tensions. In 1215 the fourth Lateran Council,

a major church conference in Rome, established the doctrine of transubstantiation, within which the bread and wine of the Lord's Supper were seen as Christ's flesh and blood. Over the next several centuries, angry priests and mob leaders repeatedly claimed that Jews desecrated wafers, seen literally as Christ's flesh, so they could persecute Jesus again. The Lateran Council also decreed that Jews should wear a special badge to differentiate them from the general population.

Other new charges and legends spread. The "blood libel" accusation—that Jews needed to kill Christian children in order to use their blood in Passover rituals—first appeared in 1144 in Norwich, England, and resurfaced throughout the 1200s. Holy Roman Emperor Frederick II investigated the charge and found it without merit, but it remained popular among those seeking a cause for mob action, as in Germany in 1298. Around 1220 an Italian wrote of meeting a Jew who had hit and insulted Jesus on the way to the crucifixion and was thus condemned to wander the world for all time and receive insults and beatings. That legend of the wandering Jew spread throughout Europe and was retold in hundreds of publications with settings frequently altered.

New charges in the 1300s made life harder for many Jews in Western Europe. In 1321 French Jews supposedly encouraged lepers to poison wells used by Christians. King Philip the Tall acknowledged the Jews' innocence but only after about five thousand Jews were killed, and the following year King Charles IV expelled those who had survived. That was only a prelude to the Black Death riots of 1348–1349, when Germans and others accused Jews of causing the bubonic plague by poisoning wells. Pope Clement VI said the Jews were innocent, but many Jewish communities already hurt by disease were wiped out by assault. Basle residents, for example, burned six hundred Jews at the stake and expelled the city's other Jews, converting the synagogue into a church and destroying the Jewish cemetery.

Jews for a time had a refuge in Muslim Spain, but Catholic rioters in Seville, Valencia, and other cities murdered thousands of Spanish Jews in 1391, and pressed others to be baptized to save their lives. Over time it became clear that many *conversos*—those baptized under pressure—and their children were continuing to practice Judaism. In 1481 Spain's Queen Isabella agreed with papal authorities on the need for an Inquisition to root out *conversos* who still practiced Judaism. From 1486 to 1490 about five thousand *conversos* went on trial: 150 "crypto-Jews" were burned at the stake, usually after torture-generated confessions. Some wealthy individuals whose lives were spared had their property confiscated, with proceeds used for financing voyages of exploration.

The end for Spanish Judaism came in 1492, when the Spanish government gave all Jews the old choice of exile or baptism under pressure. Thousands of Jews were hurriedly baptized; *conversos* largely manned Christopher Columbus's ships. At least 100,000 Jews left, many going to Portugal—where they were kicked out five years later—or heading to Muslim-controlled lands, where they generally were treated in degrading ways but allowed to survive, if they paid royally for the privilege. The Spanish government confiscated all Jewish property, ploughed under Jewish cemeteries, and either destroyed synagogues or turned them into churches or pigsties.

One city that did not expel Jews pioneered a new technique to restrict Jewish social interaction with the rest of the populace: Venice officials in 1516 began requiring Jews to live in a special area of the city where a foundry (ghetto in Italian) was located. Ghettoization also made it easier to slap on extra taxes and expropriate Jewish property, and in 1554 Pope Paul IV advised cities everywhere within Christendom to set up ghettoes.

Jews also served as sources of entertainment and objects of ritual. For two centuries, from 1466 to 1667, Rome's annual carnival entertainment prior to Lent starred eight Jews wearing only loincloths who had to run a distance of a quarter mile between jeering spectators. The spectators threw rocks and garbage at the runners and then forced rabbis and other community leaders to kiss a statue of a pig.

Living in such difficult environments over the centuries, Jews looked for alternatives to despair. Two ways became dominant. One demanded establishment of a virtual reality through Talmud study, which became a form of mental ski jumping that trained the mind to stay focused and the body to be poised yet relaxed, regardless of the winds buffeting a person in midair. Jewish boys were to study throughout the day, and adult males were to study whenever they could.

This emphasis had started early, shortly after the time of Christ. The exemplary shaper of what became Talmudic Judaism was Rabbi Yohanan ben Zakkai, said to be so righteous that he never walked more than four cubits—two yards!—

without studying and thinking about the Torah. Furthermore, rabbis taught that God honors the diligent student. *Pirke Aboth* (Sayings of the Fathers), the best-loved section of the Talmud, quotes Rabbi Nethunia stating, "Whoso receives upon himself the yoke of the Torah, from him the yoke of the kingdom and the yoke of worldly care will be removed."

Pirke Aboth also quotes Rabbi Jacob saying, "He who is walking by the way and studying, and breaks off his study and says, 'How fine is that tree . . . ,' him Scripture regards as if he had forfeited his life." It indicates that, "If even one person diligently occupies himself with the Torah, [God] appoints unto him a reward." Generation after generation, Jews studied the Talmud so much and held it in such high esteem that the Jewish vision of heaven became a place where adults, freed from having to earn a living, could study it all day long.

Major sections of the Talmud are made up of extremely specific detail about temple worship, including how to kill and dismember the animals used in sacrifice and how to arrange worship by the temple liturgical calendar. Those who studied and visualized the instructions could almost feel that they were there. Menahoth 110a of the Babylonian Talmud includes Rabbi Johanan's statement that studying the laws of temple service is the equivalent of actually carrying them out.

That raises challenging questions: Was a sacrifice studied a sacrifice made? Was the recitation of material about the sacrifices of old as meritorious as a sacrifice made in reality? Donald Akenson notes in *Surpassing Wonder* that the Babylonian Talmud even includes a passage in which

Abraham asks God (curiously, since the temple then had not yet been built) what he will do when Israel sins against him and the temple no longer exists. God says he will provide in advance for that: the Torah will describe the procedure for sacrifice, and when scholars study that, they will be forgiven their sins because it will be as if they were offering up the sacrifices physically.

The Talmud, though, is not only about a virtual reality: most of it deals with moral problems, such as the utility and legality of divorce, that persist from age to age. Study of the Talmud taught practical applications and also preempted time that could have been used to study the outside world, for that could lead to interest in Christianity. Periodically some younger Jews tried to move away from the separatist emphasis, and rabbis quashed attempts. For example, in 1305 Rabbi Shlomo Ben Aderet of Barcelona, concerned that some bright young people were stepping out, proscribed studying of philosophy and science by anyone under the age of twenty-five. His influence led to bans of that sort in many Jewish communities.

Furthermore, study of the Talmud merged with the other means Jews used to keep hope alive. They prayed for the imminent arrival of the *moshiach,* for if that occurred, study of temple sacrifices would soon move from theory to reality, as a third temple was constructed. The supply of messianic pretenders met demand. In 458 Moses of Crete said that God would part the Mediterranean Sea so that he and his followers could walk from the island to Zion. Several hundred adherents showed their faith by diving off a towering cliff into the water. Almost all of them drowned, and Moses disappeared. Around AD 700 one Abu Isa' al-Isfahani proclaimed himself the messiah, but Muslim forces wiped out his army in a mountainous battle. Abu disappeared with several diehard followers, saying he had entered a hole in the side of the mountain and would someday return.

In 1127 some Jews became destitute after incurring large debts to prepare for lavish Passover celebrations in anticipation of the messiah's arrival that year. On a mid-twelfth-century Passover evening some waited on their rooftops in the expectation that angels would pick them up and fly them to Jerusalem. Near that century's end a messiah candidate arose in Yemen and told his followers to give all their wealth to the poor. When Arabs who captured him demanded that he prove his claim, he told them that if they cut off his head, he would immediately come to life. The captors obliged, but he stayed dead.

In 1280 Abraham Abulafia, stating that he was the Son of God, headed to Rome to convert Pope Nicholas III to Judaism, but the pope had him arrested. Abulafia's followers were chagrined, and the would-be redeemer died in disappointment in 1291. In 1500 Asher Lämmlin won large support for his messiahship among both ignorant and learned Germanic Jews, but disillusionment set in two years later. Great excitement ensued in 1524 when Shlomo Molcho claimed to be the messiah, but he was burned at the stake in 1532. A claimant in Palestine, Hayyim Vital, also left his followers disgruntled.

In 1665 Eastern European Jews, stunned by Cossack attacks on them in 1648 and thereafter, pinned their hopes to Turkey's Shabbetai Zvi. Born on the ninth of Av, the anniversary of the destruction of the temple—one rabbinic tradition held that the messiah had to be born on that day—the brilliant but manic Zvi received backing from leading rabbis such as Nathan of Gaza and tens of thousands of European Jews. Zvi strode into Constantinople in 1666 saying the sultan would be impressed enough to give him authority over the land of Israel. Instead Zvi received three options: prove through miracles that you are the messiah, convert to Islam, or die. Zvi chose conversion, and a few of his supporters followed him into Islam, forming a Muslim sect that continues to this day.

Many Jews disciplined themselves with further Talmud study, but so desperate was the need that some still hoped in Zvi and awaited his second coming. In the 1750s one honored rabbi, Ya'akov Emden, accused a great Talmudic expert, Rabbi Yonatan Eybeschutz, of "secret Shabbetianism" (continued hope that Zvi was the real thing). Accusations and counter-accusations led to an uproar, and the issue was never settled.

Also during that decade, one Jacob Frank won a following for his claim to be the reincarnation of Zvi. Frank said Zvi could have displayed messianic powers had Jews repented, but they did not because they were sexually unsatisfied. Frank and his followers had orgies and sinned openly in other ways as well, saying that in the messianic time all was legitimate. He also argued that sin carried to the extreme would become repugnant, so people would then turn away from it. Rabbis, not buying that approach, excommunicated Frank.

As Frank faded from view, a new hope not based in separatism arose. In 1778, Europe's first modern Jewish school—one that taught mathematics, modern language, art, and business subjects—opened in Berlin, and five years later Moses Mendelssohn published his translation of the Torah into German. Mendelssohn argued that Jews could be both Orthodox and part of the modern world and should speak the language of the countries in which they resided. In the new world New York Rabbi Gershom Mendes Seixas received an invitation to George Washington's 1789 inaugural.

Jews demanding emancipation had to overcome the prejudices of Enlightenment leaders such as Voltaire, who hated Jews for their purported "stubbornness, their new superstitions," and for how they "surpassed all nations in impertinent fables, in bad conduct, and in barbarism." Nevertheless, the French Revolution and Napoleon's subsequent conquests brought to France and other Western European countries Jewish emancipation—total, legal equality with non-Jews.

The path was not always straight: some Germans and Danes rioted in 1819 to protest rights they said were allowing Jews to exploit others. Nevertheless, emancipation accelerated after the revolutionary upheavals of 1848–1849. From 1867 to 1874 Jews of Austria, Germany, Switzerland, and Italy received full emancipation, with ghettoes abolished. Separatists within Judaism had been dominant for centuries because there was no point in asking for admission to a club that would not accept Jews. But once emancipation opened the club in Western Europe and brought forward new options for both appeasers and transformers, separatism fell with surprising speed.

The choice became working for transformation or sliding into appeasement. Appeasers now had the opportunity to ignore the Bible and merge into an increasingly secularizing society by leaving the synagogue entirely and having no religious affiliation. Or they could become nominal Christians, with few questions asked at state churches that were quickly losing their biblical edge, and few repercussions within the fragmenting Jewish population. Some, wishing to retain some affiliation with Judaism, embraced a variety of Judaism called "Reform" that promoted worship and practice similar to that of the increasingly liberal churches of Germany or other countries.

The number of transformers also grew. Some, following in Mendelssohn's footsteps, attempted to combine Orthodox worship with involvement in broader social and political trends. Others, like Mendelssohn's grandson Felix, lived as Christians not to abandon the Bible but to transform their own communities and others by taking hold of all of it. They read the prophet Isaiah's promise from God to make Israel "a light for the Gentiles, to open eyes that are blind, to free captives from prison and to release from the dungeon those who sit in darkness" (Isa. 42:6–7). They typically hoped to bring new vitality to Christianity while liberating the minds of some of their own people.

From the eighteenth to the early twentieth centuries, though, an almost-iron curtain running from the Baltic to the Balkans divided Europe, with most Jews west of it coming to embrace modernity and most east of it becoming even more removed from the cultures that surrounded them. The Hasidic movement, rife with mysticism, grew in the mid-eighteenth century when new pogroms hit Jews in eastern Poland. The Russian Empire in 1791 completed its acquisition of much of Poland and set up a ghetto area called the Pale of Settlement; Jews could live there and nowhere else. New legislation separating Jews and Russians came in 1804.

Hungarian rabbi Moses Sofer in 1806 opened a Talmudic school and insisted that Jews have no contact with modernity. His pupils became influential throughout Eastern Europe. The Russian government tried to break Jewish culture by grabbing twelve-year-old Jewish boys and assigning them to "community service" in a peasant village for six years and then military service for the following twenty-five. Over the next three decades some forty thousand to fifty thousand boys were removed from the Jewish community in this manner, but that gross attack finally ended.

Other attacks followed, with major pogroms in 1881 and 1903. My great grandfather was killed in one. The pogroms became reported on and criticized in Western Europe, but Russian Jewish poet Haim Nahman Bialik's reaction was particularly poignant. He criticized not only the perpetrators but also Jewish men—cowards, he called them—who were unable or unwilling to fight back, often because they were engrossed in Talmud study.

In Western Europe many Jews became transformers or appeasers, although the road to freedom was twisted there as well. In 1893, anti-Semites gained some electoral success in Germany, and in 1894 the French government sent Captain Alfred Dreyfus to prison for allegedly selling military secrets to Germans; Dreyfus gained acquittal in 1906. In Eastern Europe most Jews remained in the separatist tradition, rendered romantically by Sholem Aleichem's stories about Tevye the Milkman from 1894 on. Others repudiated tradition by joining the only option that beckoned to them, revolutionary socialist parties.

The Russian Revolution of 1917 shook separatism to its core. Bolsheviks abolished the Pale of Settlement, along with all anti-Jewish laws, and many Jews had high government and Communist Party positions. Soviet Communists embraced Jews initially but condemned Judaism, and it did not take long for all expressions of Jewish culture not considered revolutionary to be made illegal. Soviet leaders of Jewish ancestry such as Trotsky, Zinoviev, and Kamenev attacked Jews and Christians, and then one another, until Josef Stalin killed all of them. (A rabbi once told the atheistic Trotsky, whose original name was Bronstein, that the Trotskys made the revolution and the Bronsteins paid the price.)

In the United States, assimilation without atheism could work: the first movie with sound, *The Jazz Singer* in 1927, showed the process. But then a hard-to-believe cautionary note blared out of Germany, as a politician fulfilled his early campaign promise to kill Jews. Adolf Hitler's creed arose not out of Christianity but out of racial theories that originated in the eighteenth-century Enlightenment and gained prominence through social Darwinism's emphasis on survival of the fittest. After Hitler gained power in 1933, his minions moved from organized rioting and the burning of Jewish books to the closing and destruction of Jewish stores and homes and eventually the murder of six million Jews.

Hitler killed Eastern European separatism by killing those who had tried to live by the Talmud, in peace, apart from the surrounding society. The last words of many Jews marched into Nazi gas chambers came from that statement of faith penned by the medieval Jewish sage Maimonides: "I believe with a full heart in the coming of the Messiah, and though he may tarry I will still wait for him." Over the opposition of some Jews who thought the return to the promised land had to await the return of the *moshiach,* Western countries tried to make restitution for the Holocaust by allowing a Jewish homeland in Israel.

Israel became a country in 1948, putting into practice a pledge made after so many went to their deaths without fighting back: "Never again." Israel fought again for its survival in 1956, 1967, and 1973, and emigration from the former Soviet Union has helped Israel's Jewish population to increase to about 4.7 million. Since the U.S. adult Jewish population is somewhat over 5 million, it's clear that Judaism once again has two main centers, as in Talmudic days when the two main centers were Palestine and Babylonia.

In both of those centers, most Jews deserted Orthodox belief and practice during the twentieth century, in a way that probably was inevitable once they took Moses Mendelssohn's advice to enter the modern world. Rabbis had no practical answer to the Jewish version of the song from early in the century, "How you gonna keep them down in the Talmud, after they've seen Pa-ree?" Persecution of Jews and Talmudic separatism had gone together, and when persecution slackened, modernity beckoned.

Talmudic rules that had seemed protective now seemed restraining. "Build community through living close together," the rabbis had counseled, and the existence of formal ghettos went along with Orthodox stipulations to live within easy walking distance of a synagogue so as not to break rules against breaking a sweat. When the external pressure that required clustering diminished, so did the internal. What had brought together those with no place else to go seemed arbitrary after new choices appeared.

The Orthodox concept of the *moshiach* also became less central to the consciousness of many emancipated Jews. Hope in the coming of a learned and great governmental/military leader grew most intense when physical life was at its worst. The *moshiach* would free humanity from war and deprivation so that people could devote all their time to the study of philosophy and to keeping God's laws. Some said that he would come if Israel repented for even a single day or observed even one (or two) Sabbaths properly. Others said he would come when a generation lost hope. But a better life in America made both repentance and hopelessness less likely for a time. In America, with opportunities in the larger world there for the taking, life in the Talmudic virtual reality was less appealing.

So throughout the twentieth century, immigrants to America who were Orthodox begat children who identified with loose constructionist interpretations of the Bible. But the rings of Saturn could not exist without Saturn; new generations did commit to a coreless religion. Conservative, Reform, and Reconstructionist Jews often begat children who, seeing Judaism as irrelevant to their lives, became scornful of it. Liberal Jewish leaders recommended clinging to customs after the thinking behind the customs was gone, but their children were watching cartoons in which cats ran off cliffs with their legs still moving through the air for a while. The plunge to earth was inevitable, and attachment to Judaism in recent decades has fallen just as sharply.

One result of that plunge is intermarriage. Half of Jews today marry non-Jews. Jewish leaders worry about this, but just as parents of the bride need to see they are not losing a daughter but gaining a son, so those concerned about Jewish loss might see Jewish gain. Christians understand God's promise to Abraham that through him all the world will be blessed as a reference to Abraham's descendant Jesus, but it can be applied secondarily to the spread of blessing through education and intermarriage.

"Jews Turning from Judaism," *The Jewish Week* recently mourned in a front-page headline. The New York newspaper reported that "42 percent of Jews who say they are Jewish by religion described themselves as secular or somewhat secular. Of those of Jewish heritage or background, it jumped to 72 percent. That's in sharp contrast to American adults nationally, just 15 percent of whom described their outlook in that way." Based on current trends, strict constructionist Judaism is growing, and liberal Judaism is diffusing into the American populace generally.

Judaism Time Line from the Destruction of the Second Temple to the Present

70 AD Romans destroy the temple in Jerusalem.

73 First Jewish revolt ends with mass suicide at Masada.

90 Christians excluded from synagogues.

135 Bar Kokhba rebellion (second Jewish revolt) ends with perhaps half a million Jews dead.

200 Mishnah (oral law, first part of Talmud) compiled under Judah HaNasi.

212 Emperor Cracalla allows all Jews within the Roman Empire to become full citizens.

306 The Council of Elvira forbids intermarriage of Jews and Christians.

325 Council at Nicea forbids Jews from trying to convert pagans to Judiasm.

439 Emperor Theodosis forbids Jews from building new synagogues or holding important positions.

500 Babylonian Talmud largely compiled and edited by this time.

519 After residents of Ravenna, Italy, burn down local synagogues, Theodoric orders the town to rebuild the synagogue at town expense.

590 Pope Gregory the Great bans forced baptism and says Jews should be tolerated.

624 Muhammad attacks and eventually annihilates Jewish Arabian tribes for refusing to convert to Islam.

712 Jews help Muslims conquer Spain.

760 Emergence of Kararite sect that emphasizes the written Hebrew Scriptures and opposes reliance on the Talmud.

807 Caliph Harun Al Rashid of Baghdad forces Jews in his domain to wear a yellow badge (and Christians a blue badge).

1070 French Jewish theologian Rashi completes his commentaries on most parts of the Bible.

1096 Soldiers of the First Crusade massacre thousands of Jews in Central European cities.

1099 Crusaders capture Jerusalem and massacre thousands of Jews there.

1195 The scholar Maimonides (Rabbi Moses ben Maimon) completes his *Guide to the Perplexed*.

1215 A Roman Catholic Church edict forces many European Jews to wear a yellow patch on their clothing.

1230 Spanish Inquisition begins investigating Jews and Christians.

1254 Jews expelled from France.

1275 King Edward of England forces Jews over the age of seven to wear a special badge.

1285 Almost two hundred Jews are burned alive at a Munich synagogue.

1348 Many Europeans blame the Black Plague on the Jews, some of whom are tortured until they "confess" poisoning wells. Thousands are burned at the stake or otherwise murdered.

1391 Spaniards destroy Jewish settlements throughout the country.

1510 Berlin residents burn thirty-eight Jews at the stake in Berlin.

1516 Venice restricts Jews to a ghetto.

1596 Amsterdam officials allow Yom Kippur services to be held for the first time in their city.

1619 Increased persecution of Jews in Persia leads many to practice Islam outwardly and Judaism in secret.

1632 The king and queen of Spain have Miguel and Isabel Rodreguese and five others burned alive in front of them. The crime: holding Jewish rites.

1649 Bogdan Chmelnitzki leads Cossacks in the murder of thousands of Polish Jews.

1760 Baal Shem Tov, founder of Hasidism, dies.

1789 New York rabbi Gershom Mendes Seixas is an honored guest at George Washington's inaugural.

1791 Russia restricts Jews to an area between the Baltic and Black seas called the "pale of settlement."

1844 Lewis Charles Levin becomes the first Jew elected to the U.S. House of Representatives.

1852 The first Jewish hospital in the United States, Mount Sinai, opens.

1870 Italy abolishes ghettos, and the Pope abolishes a six hundred-year-old edict that required Jews to attend sermons aimed at converting them.

1873 Reform Jews in the United States establish their governing body, the Union of American Hebrew Congregations.

1881 Russians and Ukrainians attack Jews in riots known as pogroms. Massive emigration of Eastern European Jews to the United States begins.

1897 In Switzerland journalist Theodor Herzl convenes the First Jewish Zionist congress.

1898 Emile Zola publishes *J'Accuse,* a defense of Captain Alfred Dreyfus, who is eventually acquitted.

1902 Russian American Jews organize the Hebrew Immigrant Aid Society.

1917 Britain's Balfour Declaration favors formation of a Jewish state in what is now Israel.

1927 The first movie with sound, *The Jazz Singer,* shows the process of Jewish assimilation at work.

1935 Nuremburg laws remove rights of Jews in Germany.

1939 First Cuban, then U.S. immigration officials do not allow entry to 907 Jewish refugees from Germany aboard the *S.S. St. Louis;* they are sent back to Europe, where many die.

1942 Nazis begin putting into practice their Final Solution, the genocide of Jews.

1948 Israel becomes a sovereign country and fights off Arab invaders.

1967 The six-day war brings all of Jerusalem and other areas under Israeli control.

1978 Isaac Bashevis Singer receives the Nobel Prize for Literature.

1989 Mass immigration to Israel from the disintegrating Soviet Union begins.

2003 Continued suicide bombings in Israel and reprisals.

Chapter Three
Hinduism's Flow

Hinduism is the world's third largest religion and the dominant one in India and Nepal; its 900 million adherents include many in Sri Lanka, Bangladesh, and other countries. Many Hindus call their faith *Sanatana Dharma,* "eternal religion," and *Vaidika Dharma,* the truth of the Vedas. The name *Hindu* may be derived from the Persian word for *Indian* or the Persian word for the Indus river, *sindhu.*

Perhaps close to one million Hindus now live in the United States, so U.S. reporters recognize Hinduism's significance both domestically and internationally. But it's hard to make any generalizations at all about Hinduism since it consists of thousands of different groups that have developed over the past three thousand years. It has no single founder, consistent theological system, central religious organization, or single system of morality. It has colorful rituals and a huge variety of gods or subgods from which to choose.

That amorphous quality is one of Hinduism's chief appeals: it appears as a laid-back faith, especially in relation to a tightly wound one like Judaism. Hinduism's appeals today include its acceptance of other religions that do not challenge Hindu presuppositions and its lack of concern with scriptural precision.

Hinduism also offers a solution to the problem of why bad things happen to good people and good things to bad: it's because we are to look at the motion picture of goodness or evil, that contains all past lives of the soul in question, and not just to the snapshot of this life. Hindus say all souls experience *samsara* or "transmigration of the soul," a long-lasting cycle of births and rebirths. Cravings, attachments, and ignorance accumulate through these perpetual rebirths, resulting in greed, hatred, and violence.

The sum of good and bad deeds is called *karma,* and karma determines where the soul will be housed in its next life. Bad deeds can cause a person to be reborn at a lower level, or even as an animal. If a person is poor in brains, looks, or money, he is paying the price for actions in a previous life. When we fight our condition rather than accept it, we upset *dharma,* the righteous order of society, and make our next incarnation even worse.

So Hinduism in one sense is individualistic and choice-oriented: every Hindu family can have its own shrine, its own worship, and its own choice of gods. At the same time it is group oriented because the gods chosen to worship are normally those of the clan or subcaste; chapter 4 discusses the caste system. Hinduism offers a choice of paths to spiritual improvement. Of the three main ones, the *Bhakti* path is the most popular today: in it a devotee chooses a personal deity and prays to it with intense love and devotion, and that deity will offer benefits in return.

Other paths are available as well. The *karma* path emphasizes action, with good things happening to a person who keeps caste regulations, performs religious rites, and offers sacrifices. (Some modern temples say that the karma path also includes actions that lead to social improvements.) The *Gyana* path emphasizes knowledge, with those walking it gaining the understanding that will allow them to move closer to deity. Through pure acts, thoughts, or devotion, Hindus believe they can be reborn at a higher level, freed from ignorance and passion.

Relax, Hindus say, when a monotheist wonders about their apparently polytheistic penchant for worshipping numerous gods and goddesses. Hindus say that when they are worshipping those small gods they are actually bowing to Brahman, the supreme god, the impersonal ultimate reality, the world soul. They say the many gods merely represent various incarnations and manifestations of the supreme god and function in a way analogous to clothes: people wear different ones in different situations. Hindus argue that their numerous names for god signify not confusion but an intimate knowledge of divinity. A favorite analogy: Eskimos have forty-eight names for snow because they know snow intimately in its variations but still understand that all snow is essentially the same.

Hindus say the existence of multiple forms of god is a tribute to god's kindness. Here's the logic: The supreme being, they say, manifests himself in different ways constantly, and those manifestations are without starting point or end. To meditate on the supreme being, man has to use his finite capabilities to absorb infinite manifestations, which is impossible. Therefore, that which is infinite appears in billions of ways to help mankind visualize it. Think of billions of photos of the same person in different poses rather than billions of different people.

Since Hindus worship multiple forms of god, they can choose the form that works best in specific instances. For example, Hindus looking for tenderness and forgiveness worship a mother form of god—Durga, Lakshmi, Saraswati, etc.—and say that in doing so they can more easily attribute those sentiments to the deity they envision. Moreover, variety is the spice of Hinduism. Urban temples in India typically have many objects of worship. Loudspeaker-blaring music, drums, food and merchandise sellers, and a variety of booths provide the backdrop for making fruit and vegetable sacrifices to major gods, popular local deities, and even dancing cobras.

Hinduism can also be optimistic because if rituals are performed correctly, gods turn into genies, ready to help their devotees. Hindus often depict subgods such as Vishnu with multiple arms or heads that allow them more opportunity to protect people. Multiple arms indicate omnipotence, dominance in all directions; multiple heads suggest omniscience. Vishnu in particular is often said to have often come to earth in avatars—various forms—so as to save humans from tyranny or natural disasters. For instance, he came in the form of a boar to destroy one demon, in a half-man, half-lion form to defeat another, and as a dwarf to beat a demon king.

The subgods are also available to help humans in other ways. Vishnu's avatars include the great hero Rama and the great dharma-establisher Krishna. Vishnu's wife Lakshmi is the goddess of wealth and is a favorite among businessmen. Brahma's wife Saraswati is the goddess of learning and often the favorite deity of students in schools and colleges. Some Hindus also worship god families, such as Rama with his brother Lakshamana and wife Sita. Some Hindus worship the most powerful goddess, Gayatri, through recitation of the Gayatri Mantra, a chant about the light of the universe.

Many Hindus describe their religion as monistic, meaning that they believe there is no essential difference between God, man, and animals. *Advaitic*—"without dualism"— Hindus believe that everything and everyone is part of god: the universe is one unitary, organic whole, with no creator/creation separation. For reasons that are unclear, all creatures at some point split off from god, and we even think that split is natural, but we will find no true, lasting happiness until we lose our individuality by becoming reabsorbed into the cosmic whole from which we came.

Other Hindus, though, subscribe to a theistic sensibility, and one group of Hindu-Christian syncretists believes that the knowledge of Christ brought to India by the apostle Thomas two decades after the death and resurrection of Jesus underlies the worship of Vishnu and Shiva that began around that time. That's an intriguing but unproven theory that adds to the difficulty of trying to put a label on Hinduism. Perhaps it should merely be called a henotheistic religion, one stressing worship of a supreme cosmic force while recognizing other gods and goddesses as facets or aspects of that supreme force.

What most Hindus agree on is the need to transcend the process of transmigration that they believe affects all living beings. They hope to be liberated from cycles of rebirth and then in some manner be united with the universal spirit, Brahman. To move toward that goal a Hindu can do good works and live as those of his caste should. He can go on pilgrimages to the holy places in India and learn through meditation, yoga, and the help of a master. Especially when he is old, he should lead an ascetic lifestyle.

Hinduism allows for many different paths to liberation. Here's one offered in the *Svetasvatara Upanishad*:

Sit upright, holding the chest, throat and head erect. Turn the senses and the mind inward to the lotus of the heart. Meditate on Brahman with the help of the syllable OM. Cross the fearful currents of the ocean of worldliness by means of the raft of Brahman—the sacred syllable OM. With earnest effort hold the senses in check. Controlling the breath, regulate the vital activities. As a charioteer holds back his restive horses, so does a persevering aspirant hold back his mind.

Retire to a solitary place such as a mountain cave or a sacred spot. The place must be protected from the wind and rain, and it must have a smooth, clean floor, free from pebbles and dust. It must not be damp, and it must be free from disturbing noises. It must be pleasing to the eye and quieting to the mind. Seated there, practice meditation and other spiritual exercises. As you practice meditation, you may see in vision forms resembling snow, crystals, smoke, fire, lightning, fireflies, the sun, the moon. These are signs that you are on your way to the revelation of Brahman.

As you become absorbed in meditation, you will realize that the Self is separate from the body and for this reason will not be affected by disease, old age or death. The first signs of progress on the path of Yoga are health, a sense of physical lightness, clearness of complexion, a beautiful voice, an agreeable odor of the person, and freedom from craving.

All that sounds good to some, but in India the odors often aren't so agreeable. For example, the question addressed to goats at thousands of folk temples in India, is, "Would you give your life for the gods?" To receive an answer, men with sharp knives drop tamerind spice on goats' heads; in response to the irritant, the goats shake their heads in what is taken as a fatal yes, and have their throats slit. At one Indian folk temple I visited, the sacrificer explained that a local god satisfied his prayer for a son, and now he must satisfy the god: "I promised, I got, and now I must do."

Large Hindu temples do not have such sacrifices, yet they are such big business that the government has taken them over, paying the salaries of both gurus and guards and collecting rents from the shops inside and outside the temple. Priests hold onto some concessions, so someone who offers fun for the whole family can do well. At one of India's largest temples, the famous Menakshi in the old pilgrimage city of Madurai, children and adults can pay two rupees (about four cents) to throw balls of butter at statues of two angry gods, Shiva and his wife Shakti, thus cooling them down.

Another Madurai-area temple has been at the same site for three hundred years but only three years ago made the big investment of putting up kid-friendly, colorfully painted giant figures linking the temple to a popular god, Ayannar. The temple priest, Ayyaavu, acknowledged frankly that "Ayannar doesn't belong here—the temple has its own mother goddesses—but, even though it's not our tradition, we wanted to have another public figure." The temple had the money to set up the statues because its village has been prosperous in recent years.

Hinduism's diversity encourages such entrepreneurial activity, but at the same time makes god-figures of choice part of the family. At the biggest Kali temple in Chennai, India, temple executive S. Bhattuchaji provided the daily feeding schedule of the temple's four-foot-tall statue of Kali, whom he called "Mother": "At 5:45 a.m. we wake Mother, wash her face, and give her a little food. At 8 we give her fruit and at 11:45 a full meal, including rice and fried vegetables, milk, honey, coconut, and curd mixed up together. You see what a good mood she is in now. She will rest, and at 4 we will wake Mother and give her a glass of coconut water along with fruit and sweets. At 6:45 we will bring more food to Mother, ring the bell, and have a big ceremony, and at 8 p.m. Mother will go to sleep."

Meanwhile villages commonly have small shrines near their boundaries dedicated to spirits of disease and illness. These spirits need to be appeased by prayers and offerings, such as food or pieces of red cloth. Other spirits that demand propitiation include poison deities, tiger deities, and snake deities. Some spirits are seen as living in old trees or at crossroads; deities known as *kshetrapalas* guard crops.

Again, pinning down what is Hindu belief, rather than respect for tradition, is difficult. Many Hindus express ease about doctrine, along with a willingness to believe in astounding spiritual activities; for example, many Hindus do not oppose the idea of resurrection because Hindus say a truly advanced Yogi could do that. Hindus quote liberally from Jesus' comments about love and peace; some say that "Christianity is modified Hinduism," and state that between the ages of thirteen and thirty-one Jesus went to India. Hindus who write about Jesus, though, commonly leave out his tough-minded expressions of God's holiness and are hostile to his claims that there is one way to God.

Hinduism, in short, says that there are many ways to God, and many people find them attractive. Furthermore, Hinduism is a visual faith, with many idols; temples in India do not shy away from calling their statues "idols," giving devotees a tangible object for worship. Swami Vivekananda's explanation is classic: "If a person wants to drink milk, he uses a cup as he cannot drink it directly. For the quivering and unsteady mind, there should be a visible form or a symbol, the idol, so that it becomes a foundation for his adoration. The idol form of God is akin to a vessel which enables a man to drink the milk." To use an American metaphor, we commonly expect small children to need training wheels as they learn to ride a bicycle. It does seem strange that for many Hindus who line up to feed idols, the training wheels stay on for life.

Christians and Jews tend to ask lots of questions about how life began; most Hindus do not. Hinduism proclaims no creation as such because the universe goes through endless cycles of creation and destruction. The base unit to compute the length of a cycle is the Mahayuga, which is 4.3 million earthly years. One day of Brahma (a cosmic day) consists of 1000 Mahayugas, as does a cosmic night, so each is 4.3 billion earthly years long. Some scientists who like long time spans in which evolution could work have harkened to Hindu chronology.

But there's more: the standard Hindu explanation is that at the beginning of each cosmic day all embodied beings come into existence from undifferentiated god stuff; a soul is reborn many times during a cosmic day. At cosmic nightfall souls merge back into the cosmos. A cosmic year includes 12 cosmic months of 30 cosmic days, and the cosmos lasts for 100 of them; multiply out those figures and the life of the cosmos equals 311 trillion and 40 billion earth years. At the end of the cosmos, a new one emerges and lasts for another 100 cosmic years. This process goes on without end.

The size of the Hindu big tent echoes the vastness of time. Hinduism has room for thousands of religious sects and scriptures that have grown and developed in a continuous flow for several thousand years. The Vedas include over 100,000 verses, the Upanishads (books that emphasize the unity of the individual soul and the universal spirit or Brahman) over 200,000, and that's just the beginning of Hindu knowledge. Hindus say their Brahmanas (books explaining how rituals should be performed), Aranyakas (mystical texts), and Samhitas (deity-praising mantras) are *shruti,* messages divinely revealed to early sages and passed by word of mouth from generation to generation.

Many Hindus show an ease about learning or even knowing their scriptures that is far different from the intense emphases of Jews and Christians. The Rig-Veda, the earliest Hindu scripture, may have originated before 1000 BC but was not written down until about AD 1400, so some question its overall validity. About 10 percent of the lines of the epic *Mahabharata* are in question. But many Hindus do not seem to care because with a vast number of scriptures to choose from, particular lines don't seem all that important.

That vast corpus of Hindu lore places great authority in the hands of the gurus (*gu* means darkness and *ru* light, so a *guru* gives light that drives away spiritual darkness). Gurus have spent years reading many of the Hindu scriptures. (The Bible, containable in one volume, lends itself to what is sometimes called "the priesthood of all believers." Laymen can readily read and study the whole volume so that while they look to ministers and commentators for help, they are not hopelessly outclassed in knowledge.

Priests are also in charge of an enormous number of rituals said to direct spiritual entities and forces of nature. Offerings, pilgrimages, wearing of a sacred thread, and so on are seen as vital to the development of higher thinking. Rural areas commonly have a variety of *grama-devatas*, village gods and goddesses; some are a male form of Shiva, but most are female. The patron goddess of a village is seen as in charge of fertility, so women wanting to be pregnant will pray to her and promise a gift—perhaps a sari or a chicken—when a child is born. All newborns are taken to the shrine of the local goddess to receive a blessing.

With freedom to worship a chosen god also comes fear: Hindus know they have many gods (or aspects of god) to propitiate, but how do they know that they've chosen the right one?

In practice most Hindus simplify what would be otherwise maddening complexity: they go with the flow, doing what their clan or subcaste mandates. That may involve devotion to one of the major gods, like Vishnu or Shiva, and also local deities. Here's one account from a young Hindu about consecrating a family *murti* of Ganesha (son of Shiva and the god of good luck): "The day before the festival my father and I went to the sculptor, who makes clay *murti* of different gods and goddesses for religious occasions. We paid forty rupees for our *murti,* which had been ordered two months in advance. We brought the *murti* home and placed it in a copper tray on a small stool in the alcove. After the decorated frame was put in place and the electric light under the alcove switched on, the smiling Ganesha could be seen clearly, even across the front courtyard. . . .

"As Guruji [a local priest] chanted the appropriate mantras, I did the various rituals." Rituals include sprinkling rice grains on the *murti,* touching the feet of the *murti* with a wet flower, placing fresh fruit and coins before the *murti,* and so on. The young Hindu then said,

"I offer worship to god Ganesha, according to our family traditions, with my limited knowledge and with whatever is available, in order to . . . fulfill the dreams and desires of all my relations assembled here, to ward off all evil from our lives and to secure well-being, stability, long life and prosperity for all.'"

Many of Hinduism's rituals exist as ways for individuals to protect themselves against the wrath of some god. For example, many Hindus believe that bathing in one of seven sacred rivers in India can win them karmic merit. Hindu rituals also include clockwise walking around shrines so that a shrine is always on the walker's right side. Many Hindus believe that the right side of the body is spiritually purer than the left; the right hand is always used for eating, making religious offerings, and passing money to others.

Many types of ritual purifications are required during the day and especially before worship. Orthodox Hindus believe that impure thoughts lead to the formation of evil vapors in the mouth, leaving the mouth and its saliva unclean; uttering Vishnu's name three times before sipping water helps. Food left over from a meal is ritually impure, as is food that has been touched or smelled by another human being.

Since there is no clear human/animal divide, Hindus also have animal deities. Airavat is the four-tusked king-god of elephants, who emerged out of water when gods churned the ocean. The bird-god Garuda has the head and wings of an eagle, often on a man's body. Garuda is often depicted as carrying Vishnu on its back and is worshipped as a remover of obstacles. Shesh Neg, the serpent god, is the king over Patal, infernal regions. During intervals of creation Vishnu is said to sleep on its coils. Kamdhenu, the sacred cow god, also emerged from ocean-churning and is said to grant all wishes and desires; she is the mother of all cows. And so on.

Hindus have sacred cows for many reasons. Cow's milk is revered as akin to mother's milk, so Hindus compare the slaughter of a cow to matricide. Curds and ghee (clarified butter) are traditionally used in sacrifices, so ghee (and the cow from which it comes) is seen as the root of sacrifice. Gods like sacrifices, so cows are essential. Cows are seen as the "greatest givers on this earth today," and they are a "complete ecology, a gentle creature and a symbol of abundance." Many Hindus say that cows are sanctifying creatures who represent the highest energy in the universe and that a person who kills a cow or eats beef is said to rot in some form of hell for as many years as there are hairs on a cow.

Just as Hindus do not have a clear human-animal divide, so a lack of clear lines makes it difficult to define the extent of Hindu denominations. The largest one is probably Vaishnavism, with Vishnu regarded as the ultimate hero-god who comes to earth in one of his ten incarnations whenever *dharma* (eternal order and righteousness) is threatened. Followers of Shaivism, the second most popular belief, see Shiva as the leading manifestation of God: some call him the destroyer of evil, some just the destroyer, and some are particularly moved by the eroticism that is part of Shiva's edgy charm.

Shiva has 1,008 names in all, as does his wife, Shakti. When the emphasis is on her tender kindness, Shakti goes by Parvati or Sati. When the emphasis is on terror and destruction, she goes by Durga or Kali (referred to in *Indiana Jones and the Temple of Doom*). But whatever her name, Shaktas—those who worship Shakti as the supreme mother and creator/defender of the world—form the third largest group of Hindus. Other Hindus, as individuals or in clans, choose a particular god or goddess as their *ishta-devata* (personal deity) and offer it special prayers and worship, much as the ancient Greeks did.

This variety may leave individuals adrift; historically in Indian village life, individuals have worshipped whatever their subcaste and community put before them, but as India urbanizes and Hindus outside India have more choice of where to go and what to affirm, individual Hindus worry that they have chosen poorly. And yet the word *individual* itself suggests a sub-Hindu pattern of thought: the theological goal of many Hindus, if they think about their beliefs, is to lose their individuality and flow into the monistic ocean.

Unlike Christianity, Islam, and Judaism, which include concepts of personal immortality, Hindus are to seek suprapersonal immortality, with individuals merged into "ultimate being." That road to merger is a long and winding one, though, as a person may be reborn into a higher or lower life form, depending on karma. Devout Hindus today still believe that a soul is reborn again and again until enlightened and liberated from rebirth, at which time what was an individual enters a state of ultimate bliss (*moksha*) and becomes one with the ultimate, but that does mean the extinguishing of personality.

Orthodox Hindus oppose abortion, believing that unborn humans deserve protection. Abortion is seen in Hindu scriptures as *garha-batta* (womb-killing) and *bhroona hathya* (killing the undeveloped soul). Abortion at any stage of fetal development has serious karmic consequences. A hymn in the Rig Veda pleads for protection of unborn children. The Kaushitaki Upanishad draws a parallel between abortion and killing parents. The Atharva Veda notes that the *brunaghni* (fetus slayer) is among the greatest of sinners. Gandhi said that in a good Indian state it's "as clear as daylight that abortion would be a crime."

Yet the concept of *samsara* (recycling of lives) leads to some devaluation of life. Katha Upanishad 2.19, written perhaps twenty-five hundred years ago, proclaimed, "If the slayer thinks he slays/ If the slain thinks he is slain,/ Both these do not understand:/ He slays not, is not slain." The thought of only one life to live on earth concentrates the mind, but Hinduism's two most beloved epics, the *Mahabharata* (Story of the War of the Bharatas) and the *Ramayana* (Story of Ram), both emphasize the karmic cycle. Both of these epics, sometimes called the founding pillars of Hinduism, emphasize episodes in the lives of the great warriors and could provide justification for war.

The *Mahabharata* tells of how long ago the Kauravas hated their cousins, the Pandavas, and fooled them into playing a game of dice with high stakes. Winning by cheating, the Kauravas claim all the wealth and land of the Pandavas, and drive them into the forest for fourteen years of exile. When the Pandavas return after the fourteen years agreed-upon time the Kauravas refuse to part with any of their land, and the Pandavas decide to fight.

Krishna, king of a nearby region but actually a major god, tries to be a peacemaker but cannot overcome the inflamed relations. When war seems inevitable, Krishna gives the two camps a choice—one can have his impressive army, the other his guidance. The Kauravas, believing in man's strength, choose the army. The Pandavas, who know Krishna's real identity, chose godly wisdom, and Krishna becomes the chariot driver of Pandava leader Arjuna.

With the battle about to begin, Arjuna is so dismayed at the thought of killing his relatives and teachers on the other side that he refuses to fight and throws away his weapons. But Krishna tells Arjuna that he is deluded to be laid low by such transient concerns and instructs him to fight. Arjuna does and the Pandavas win, with thousands left dead on the battlefield. The poetic conversation between Arjuna and Krishna makes up the *Bhagavad Gita* (Song of the Lord), the most-read part of the *Mahabharata*. Krishna tells Arjuna, "You grieve over those who should not be grieved . . . . Wise men do not grieve over the dead or the living," since souls transmigrate from one body to another and eventually become part of the cosmic whole.

The *Ramayana*, also well-known, has as its hero Rama (as in the chant, "Hare Rama Hare Krishna"). It begins with

Ravana, the tyranical ruler of Lanka in southern India, persecuting righteous Hindus. Vishnu comes to earth as one of his avatars—Rama, son of a northern Indian king—with the goal of showing mankind the importance of upholding *dharma,* no matter what. Rama's charm, humility, and friendliness make him a beloved prince, and he marries Princess Sita, also the child of a king and also a godly incarnation.

Rama's old human father, Dasharatha, wants Rama to become king, but one of the king's three wives has once saved his life, and he has said he would grant her any two requests. Her requests turned out to be that her son become king, with Rama banished to the forest. The king is bound by the promise he has made, and Rama, having the right stuff, does not complain but heads immediately into exile, with Sita accompanying him. The old king dies of grief and Rama heads south, where persecution rages.

Rama, Sita, and friends spend ten years living ascetically in then-forested Southern India, during that time fighting and winning several wars with the tyrant Ravana and protecting good Hindus from persecution. Ravana battles back by kidnapping and imprisoning Sita with the goal of forcing her into adultery, but she, hardly eating anything, meditates on a rescue by her husband. Lust-blinded Ravana keeps trying, but Sita becomes a symbol of chastity and devotion.

Rama comes to the rescue and has his small army attack Ravana's mighty force. After a terrible war Rama singlehandedly defeats the enemy army and kills Ravana, thus ending the suffering of devout Hindus and gaining renewed union with his wife. Like the *Mahabharata,* the *Ramayana* shows that the duty of a royal hero is to preserve and develop harmonious social order—*dharma*. These key stories have had influence, and the argument that killing is not slaying, since only the body can be destroyed, has been used as justification for both assassination plots and military adventures. Americans often think of Hinduism as a laid-back religion of nonviolence, but a religion that doesn't prune itself has all kinds of strange growths. We'll look at some in the next chapter.

Hinduism Glossary

Advaita Nonduality, the belief that god and living creatures such as man are all of the same essence.

Agni The Hindu god of fire.

Ahimsa "Noninjury" in Sanskrit, the principle that a person should do no harm.

Atman An individual's essence, which many Hindus believe is part of Brahman.

Aum (or om) A meditational monosyllable that has become Hinduism's most famous mantra, since it is seen as symbolic of Brahman.

Avatar A god incarnated in an earthly form, generally that of a human or animal. Vishnu's two main avatars were Krishna and Rama.

Bhagavad-Gita The section of the Mahabharata in which Krishna reveals himself to Arjuna and describes how man should live.

Bhakta A worshipper of a god or goddess.

Bhakti Devotion to a god or goddess.

Brahman The Ultimate Force that makes the cosmos function.

Brahmin The highest Hindu caste, from which priests come.

Dalits Untouchables, those who are beneath the four established castes.

Devas Gods or celestial beings.

Dharma Righteous way of living as enjoined by the sacred scriptures; virtue.

Durga Goddess of retribution and a wife of Shiva.

Ganesha The god of good fortune; the elephant-headed son of Shiva who removes barriers and brings success to his followers.

Guru A teacher considered to be wise.

Hatha Yoga Yoga devoted to controlling body movements; a small part of yoga, but the only kind familiar to many Americans.

Ishvara "Lord," used in referring to Vishnu or other gods who are seen as representing the Ultimate Force.

Jati One of the thousands of subcastes that comprise the four major castes plus the untouchables.

Jnana Knowledge or wisdom.

Jnana Yoga The way for disciples to learn the true nature of existence and unite themselves with Brahman.

Kali A destructive goddess, one of the wives of Shiva. often depicted as wearing a necklace of human skulls and holding weapons from which blood drips.

Kama Pleasure, including sexual pleasure, which is to be grabbed onto in a nonattached way.

Karma The sum of actions in a life that determines the high or low place of rebirth.

Krishna An avatar of Vishnu.

Kshatriya The caste (second in rank) of warriors, leaders, and government officials.

Lakshmi Goddess of prosperity.

Lingam A tall, upright stone that often symbolizes a phallus, denoting Shiva's power.

Mahabharata Epic about Krishna and the battle of the Pandu brothers against their Kuru cousins.

Maharishi Great sage.

Mantra Sacred syllable, word, or sequence of sounds which devotees may repeat for hours.

Maya "Illusion," which is what the cosmos is, but it's all we can see.

Moksha Liberation from the *samsara* cyle of death and rebirth.

Murti Idol.

Puja An offering of same kind (generally food, flowers, or praise) to a god.

Puranas Writings from around 500 AD about the exploits of Hindu gods and goddesses.

Rama The popular hero god who is an avatar of Vishnu and whose story is told in the Ramayana.

Sadhu A person who renounces life, family, work, and other activities so as to become a moksha-seeking wanderer.

Samadhi The state of superconsciousness where absoluteness is said to be experienced.

Samsara The cycle of death and rebirth, based on individuals' souls transmigrating to new bodies after death occurs.

Sanatana Dharma The Hindu name for Hinduism.

Shaivism Belief in Shiva and worship of him through rituals.

Shiva/Siva One of the two main gods of Hinduism: The *sh* pronunciation is typical of Northern India, the *s* of Southern.

Shudra Literally, slave: the fourth and lowest Hindu caste.

Twice-born Description of someone from the upper three castes who has gone through a coming-of-age ceremony, generally at age twelve.

Upanishads A group of ancient Hindu scriptures that examine the relationship between man and the Ultimate Force.

Vaishnavism Worship of Vishnu, which often means worship of one of his avatars, particularly Rama and Krishna.

Vaishya The third Hindu caste, made up of the merchants, traders, farmers, and craftsmen.

Varna Hindu term for caste, the social division into which a person is born.

Vedas The oldest collection of Hindu sacred texts, said to be written by 500 BC.

Vishnu Main Hindu god who cares for mankind and sends avatars; Krishna and Rama are best known.

Yoga Union with the Supreme Force and the discipline that makes for such union, such as meditation and body exercises.

Chapter Four

Untouchable Problems

The great civil-rights conflict throughout the coming decade and perhaps the entire twenty-first century is the battle in India of 240 million Dalits (untouchables) to break out of two thousand years of subservience. India's caste system is not just a social problem for the world's second largest nation but a theological problem for the world's third largest religion, since Hindu belief underlies the system and keeps most of those at the bottom from pushing for change.

The racial problems of Hinduism became real to me one Saturday evening in the thatched-hut village of Manapakkam in Southeastern India. At a small cinder-block building with a stucco finish and a sign proclaiming Praise Evangelical Church, I saw and heard three hundred children from the untouchable caste sitting in rows on the concrete floor and squealing in delight, for it was time for a Bible club jamboree.

The children sat in rows on the cement floor facing a little stage on which they took turns reciting Bible memory verses, offering welcome dances and skits about the Good Samaritan and other Bible stories, and singing as loudly as they could into a novelty item, a microphone. They then ate generous portions of rice with bits of meat placed on banana leaves in front of them.

They also wanted to be touched. They crowded around American visitors who patted them on their heads. They wanted to shake hands, again and again. Part of it was fascination with odd-looking folks from the other side of the world. But part of their interest, I learned, lay in being treated as fellow human beings, not subhuman inferiors.

The next night came more of the same at Peniel Prayer House in another village, Mettukuppam, where few men live beyond fifty years and most houses have illicit stills where they brew alcohol to raise some money and drown many sorrows. Two hundred children sat patiently on the cement floor of a 25-by-50-foot structure and then laughed uproariously as kids in skits staggered around like drunks; they've obviously observed a lot of that.

Again the orderliness of the kids was impressive. No one ate until all were served rice with vegetables and a bit of meat, topped by a whole hard-boiled egg, a rare treat. Using their right hands only—left hands serve for indelicate tasks—they worked their rice into balls and scooped it into their mouths. Their good cheer in slums far poorer than any in the United States reflected a willingness not to dwell on the bad but to enjoy the good.

The following night brought a visit to a Bible club in Kettackanappie, a village near the city of Bangalore. The first two programs are several years old and hold their gatherings in local church buildings, but this three-month-old program has only a twelve-by-twelve-foot rented cowshed into which thirty-five children crammed. Parents pushed against the door so they could hear their children reciting Genesis 1:1, "In the beginning God created the heavens and the earth," a key line in any culture and especially in a Hindu one that claims there was no beginning.

Why were these children untouchables? What about adult untouchables in the poor, Anakaputhur section of Chennai, the city formerly known as Madras? Many women in that area had been economically dependent on tannery work for twenty-five rupees a day plus the likelihood that their hands would be ruined by acid and their hearts sickened by a daily dose of managerial abuse. But six years ago a Christian couple started a needlepoint enterprise where young women receive two dollars a day (about 100 rupees) making exquisite tablecloths and napkins, as one of them reads the Bible out loud.

Why were Christians willing to touch the untouchables? How had the caste system arisen within Hinduism, and why did it remain long after comparable instances of racism—like slavery in the U.S. and other countries—were no more? We could look at aspects of contemporary Indian culture, but Dalits themselves often speak of the theology. Udit Raj at a congressional human-rights hearing offered a radical but apparently accurate appraisal: "The untouchables have been convinced to live this dehumanized life because they are said to be condemned to it by the desire of the gods. Accordingly, it is considered good if they suffer because their present suffering will liberate them in the next life."

In recent years some upper-caste Hindus have refused to defend untouchability and have argued that helping the poor improves the karma of the helper without reducing that of the person helped—but that novel interpretation is up against many centuries of caste predestination. The caste system probably originated with the subjugation by lighter-skinned Aryan invaders from the north and west of India's native, darker-skinned Dravidians. Aryans produced the Law of Manu, said to be over two thousand years old but certainly over one thousand, which proclaims the different tasks for the four main castes—Brahman, Kshatriya, Vaishya, and Shudra. Brahmans were to be priests and teachers, Kshatriyas officials and soldiers, and Vaishyas merchants and farmers.

The *Mahabharata* further spelled out the work of the lowest-caste Shudra: "To become the servant of the other three orders. . . . By such service of the other three a Shudra may obtain great happiness. He should wait upon the three other classes according to their order of seniority. A Shudra should never amass wealth, lest by his wealth he makes the numbers of the three superior classes obedient to him. By this he would incur sin. . . . Shudras should certainly be maintained by the other orders. Worn out umbrellas, turbans, beds and seats, shoes, and fans, should be given to the Shudra servants, [and also] torn clothes which are no longer fit for wear."

A Shudra was to have total loyalty to those who gave him torn clothes: He "should never abandon his master whatever the nature or degree of the distress into which the latter may fall. If the master loses his wealth, he should with excessive zeal be supported by the Shudra servant. A Shudra cannot have any wealth that is his own. Whatever he possesses belongs lawfully to his master." Shudra were also treated as spiritually inferior: as the Mahabharata puts it, a Shudra "is not competent to utter swaha and sadha or any other Vedic mantra."

The caste system received additional theological backing from India's leading medieval philosopher, Sankara (788–820), who insinuated that Brahmins are gods who alone understand the way things truly are. Most people see the phenomena that occur around us as real, but they are deluded: "This entire apparent world in which good and evil actions are done, etc., is a mere illusion . . . and does in reality not exist at all." Brahmins, though, have the intellectual qualities to gain true understanding: For them, "The Self is within, the Self is without, the Self is before and the Self is behind. The Self is on the right hand, the Self is on the left, the Self is above and the Self is below."

Some later theologians denounced Sankara; Ramanuja, India's second most famous philosopher, denounced Sankara's "fictitious foundation of altogether hollow and vicious arguments . . . from one whose intellect is darkened and who has no insight into the meaning of words and sentences." Ramanuja in the eleventh century emphasized not the path of knowledge but a combination of *bhakti* (personal effort toward devotion) and *prapatti* (complete dependence on the divine). His disciples split into two camps: the *markara* (monkey hold) school, which held that adherents had to make an effort to grab onto deity, much as young monkeys need to cling to their mothers, and the *marjara* (cat) school, which held that devotees are passive recipients of grace, with the Cosmic Force grabbing souls by the scruff of the neck as a cat does kittens.

Crucially, though, neither Ramanuja nor his followers tried to change the caste system; grace took hold after death and in the next life, not in this one. Later India's third most famous philosopher, Madhva, gave a thirteenth century list of universal commands for all castes: "Do not lie, slander no one, use no harsh words, do not talk idly, do not steal, do not commit adultery, do not kill, do not think evil thoughts, do not hate, do not be proud." But what Sankara, Ramanuja, and Madhva, despite their great philosophical differences, all had in common was a defense of the caste system and its claim that only Brahmins could enter into true knowledge of the world.

Castes and subcaste status passed from one generation to the next, with sons almost always following the occupations of their fathers. Over time a fifth caste developed from those who were stuck with doing unclean jobs, such as removing dead animals and tanning leather. These lowest caste members were said to be ritually unclean and "untouchable." Those on top felt they could be polluted by being near those at the bottom, eating food touched by them, or drinking from the same well as them. In some parts of India, even a contact with the shadow of an untouchable was considered polluting.

India legally abolished the caste system in 1949, but custom is generally stronger than law, and castes remain a significant force throughout India. Traditionally each Indian Hindu also belongs to one of the thousands of Jats (communities), grouped into the four castes plus the fifth, "untouchable" group. A person's Jat determines the range of jobs for which he is eligible and the spouses he might be able to marry.

Customs still prohibit persons of different groups from eating or drinking with one another. Most Hindus invite only fellow caste members to meals in homes. At a wedding feast different castes eat at the same time but in different rows. It is now illegal in India to discriminate against a person because of caste, and change has come within large urban areas. In some rural areas, though, almost nothing has changed, as some press accounts have shown.

For example, an evocative Associated Press article in 2001 told this story:

At the end of a network of dusty lanes in Trilokpuri, a suburb on the outskirts of the Indian capital, a scavenger lugs home a plastic bucket of water for her family. It is dusk, and Birum and her two daughters have spent the day collecting used plastic bags from rotting waste in city dumps. The mother and daughters are filthy and hungry—yet they cannot bathe or cook with water from a tap near their home. . . .

"That's the tap for the upper castes. We are not allowed there," the 33-year-old Birum says as she sits on the dirt floor making bread on a coal-burning stove. Although water is supplied by municipal authorities, the few public taps in this shantytown of nearly 10,000 people are divided along caste lines. Taps for the lower castes are nearly a half-mile away, and the water barely trickles. Birum is a Dalit, the lowest rank [within the caste system that] was described in Hinduism's ancient sacred text, the Rig Veda, as a social order intended to maintain harmony in society.

The AP story noted that discrimination based on caste is now outlawed in India, yet "the practice pervades society" to such an extent that only 3 percent of the Dalits have benefited from legal changes. Many say the caste system is similar to racism, but Hindu religious leaders who criticized racism in the United States support India's caste system as theologically correct. The article ended with a note that, despite having the law on their side, "Dalits rarely file complaints with the police. 'Who can we complain to? And what will happen when we return to the village? I tell my sons, just keep quiet. This is a curse on our lives,' said 71-year-old Kishan Chand." Karma rules.

Ellis Cose, author of the book *Color-Blind: Seeing Beyond Race in a Race-Obsessed World,* also noted the theological underpinnings of continued casteism: "Intractable as prejudice sometimes seems in America, at least here it isn't rooted in religion; at least in taking on bigotry, we are not taking on God. Indeed, it is just the opposite." He observed that "Dalits are relegated in Hinduism to an almost sub-human niche beneath the formal caste system."

Although Indian leaders talk of how that has changed in the half century since Indian independence, Cose wrote that his interviewees "swore that, particularly in rural areas, Dalits continue to be treated like dirt." He noted that even when disasters leave many dead or homeless, "villages have created segregated tent camps." He told of one Dalit who "had been literally beaten to death for questioning an order from his higher caste boss. I heard similar stories elsewhere, as well as repeated complaints Dalits were not allowed to go into the community temple or draw water from the village well."

A story that's made its way around India indicates the extent of deception and self-deception. A prominent Dalit politician returns to his small village to open a hospital and receives a hero's welcome from those who once shunned him. After a fancy lunch he is preparing to leave when another Dalit comes into the room through a back door. The politician says, "You don't have to come in by the back way now. I was once like you, and see what I have made of myself." The other replies, "I just came to get my plates. They borrowed them to serve you your lunch."

The struggle of the Dalits today has its parallels with the U.S. civil rights struggle of the 1950s and 1960s, but one difference is immense. The U.S. movement, propelled by groups such as the Southern Christian Leadership Conference, emphasized the biblical sense of equality. Martin Luther King Jr. preached about God offering salvation to people of all races. He gained support from many whites who understood that as well.

Reverend King also taught that Christianity offers truth both for the next world and this one: not only "pie in the sky when we die," to quote one Marxist attack on biblical faith but increased spiritual and psychological health in this one. He taught that economic advance would also come as racism decreased and as individuals chose long-term advancement over harmful drives for immediate gratification.

In India, though, vast numbers believe that Dalits are inferior by nature. Many see the poor as suffering in accordance with their karma, paying the price for misdeeds of a past life. Many Dalits themselves believe that their karma for this life is already determined, and that submissiveness now will give them a better rebirth.

Dalits who convert to a belief system not based on karma, though, are unlikely to remain submissive. If they convert to Christianity, they are even likely to see themselves, like other men and women, created in the image of a wonderful God who does great things, and thus they can see themselves as able to do great things as well. At the least they will be accepted as brothers rather than inferiors. Fearing that millions will flee Hinduism, Indian leaders intent on closing the escape hatch have passed laws in several states that forbid conversion when it leads to any material improvement.

Those laws are controversial, particularly since they seem to violate Article 25 of the Indian constitution, by which an Indian citizen has the right to embrace any faith and practice any religion in the way its scriptures demand. But Article 25 has an elastic clause: Indian government officials can say no to any exercise of a basic right if it creates a problem in health, public order, or morality. That clause makes sense in some situations: the government might want to restrict temple or church activities during a cholera epidemic or forbid shrine prostitutes.

Recently, though, the elastic has been stretched to prohibit "allurement," the granting of any material benefit for conversion; since Dalits in India generally can work only in the lowliest occupations, when they convert to a faith which does not discriminate against them, they have the opportunity to do better. That means Christian missionaries can readily be accused of coercing "conversion" by offering opportunity, especially when they have to file forms regarding any converted person that gives the "occupation and monthly income of the person converted." If a Dalit previously restricted to dirty work gets a better job with an improved income, government officials can cry allurement.

U.S. reporters have shown little understanding of the economic function of anticonversion legislation. For example, an Associated Press article about Tamil Nadu's law framed it positively as a way of bringing peace to a "multifaith society where violence among the followers of rival beliefs is all too common." The AP article briefly quoted a Christian critic and a Muslim opponent of the new law but ended with more spin: One of Indian Hinduism's senior holy men, Jayendra Saraswathi, said a ban on conversions should be enacted nationally. "'It is a pity that even after 50 years of independence, conversions are taking place in the name of God,' he said." AP also sympathetically quoted "a former Supreme Court judge, V. Ramaswamy, [who] said the law did not violate religious freedoms. 'On the contrary, it only goes to strengthen that right by ensuring that the individual is not forced or lured into practicing some other religion instead of his own.'"

American journalists need to do better than that, and they can. They should learn from Indian journalists who have stressed the irony of governmental desires purportedly to protect the Dalits from conversion pressure. P. Radhakrishnan wrote in a major daily newspaper, *The Hindu,* "When the state has hardly any concern for [Dalits], and they are still victims of untouchability and social ostracism, why should it be a stumbling block to their regeneration with the help of other religions?" Columnist Kancha Ilaiah raised the question of whether Brahmins who want to hold onto lower caste followers will "resolve the caste contradiction within Hindu religion," and observed "no indications that Hinduism will allow spiritual democracy within its structure."

Dalits are not even allowed to set foot in traditional Hindu temples, but some temples owned and operated by sudras (the Hindus one step up from untouchability) have set up separate and unequal Dalit wings. Some untouchables also have set up their own temples. Dalit P. Narayanan, son of the priest at the Muniyandi Temple Kosakulam, near Madurai, will inherit the post from his father, but he also has a bachelor's degree in finance and coolly appraises the economics of temple life. His is a low-budget temple with expenses of only fifty thousand rupees per year (about

$1,100) and a reliance on small donations, often less than a rupee, from the agricultural laborers who attend.

Unlike the big, Brahmin-run temples, Muniyandi owns no land outside the temple grounds and is not allowed to make lucrative arrangements for the sale of tamerind pods. Muniyandi also recently ended its big moneymaker, an annual bull-catching event, because of concerns about torturing bulls and putting human lives in jeopardy. Now the temple's budget depends on the number of people it can attract to its dance competition, team games, and running events.

So separate but unequal temples of all kinds now exist, but the dehumanization said to be decreed by the gods remains, with many Hindus seeing acquiescence as good because current suffering leads to better placement in the next life. Submissiveness creates good karma. That same theology has been used to hold down women, with statements from the *Mahabharata* such as these: "There is nothing else that is more sinful than women. Verily, women are the root of all faults. . . . Jealousy, hatred, pride, hypocrisy, suspicion, intolerance and crookedness are some of the common evil qualities in women."

The prejudice is clear: "Women are fierce. . . . Men should feel no affection for them. Nor should they entertain any jealousy on account of them. Having a regard only for the considerations of virtue, men should enjoy their society, not with enthusiasm or attachment but with reluctance and absence of attachment. By acting otherwise, a man is sure to meet with destruction." Such prejudice has led to customs now rarely followed, such as the burning of widows, and others perhaps followed more than ever, such as battering of wives, who find ways to strike back.

One way is at places like Pandi Koil in Madurai, the great pilgrimage city of southeastern India. Three decades ago this temple was merely a small shack in a sacred grove owned by five families. Then, slowly, it gained a reputation as a place where women, usually in their 40s, could come to twist and shriek, in the assumption that they are temporarily possessed by a male god named Pandi. Some women shave their heads and apply sandalwood paste. Others assert that they have been seized by Pandi and must come to the temple every Tuesday and Friday for the next ten weeks.

The temple has become so popular that five years ago it installed railings like those at theme park rides to keep the crowds in check. Many women troubled by stomach pains or a colicky child vow to Pandi, "If you cure me of this, I will come to your temple." If the pains or the crying go away, they come to a place where they don't have to respond to the entreaties of husbands or fathers but can wail and flail all they want. They don't seem so possessed, though, that they are unaware of their immediate environment: one shrieker walking backward stopped an inch short of bumping into me.

Branches of Pandi Koil have now sprung up all over the Indian state of Tamil Nadu, as have more than one hundred congregations of women called Adhiparashakti. In traditional Hinduism women are not permitted to offer puja (worship) in a temple's holy of holies, but in this new demonination *only* women do puja. Ironically, a man, Bangaru Adigalar, now sixty-three, established the congregation: His devotees address him as "Mother," say he has merged with the goddess Shakti, and speak proudly of their new opportunity to offer temple worship themselves.

This concept has caught on so quickly that one group in Madurai, which until recently owned merely a memorial stone and several bells, now has a small building decorated with two calendars featuring Adigalar portraits and six other pictures of the guru that depict him with a halo and red marks on his hands and feet. The group plans to erect a new, elaborate temple at a cost of five million rupees, or about $109,000. That's a lot in an economy where one hundred rupees per day, little more than two dollars, is a decent income.

Tiny women also face problems, as the district-by-district birth figures for South India indicate. Usilampatti in December 2002 had 910 male births and only 690 female ones. Chellampatti had 848 male births and 623 female ones. And so it goes: Boy babies are desired, girl babies despised and, probably one out of four times, killed. Most Indians desire male sons for both theological and economic reasons. Only sons can perform the funeral rites that purportedly help give souls safe passage to good rebirths. Only a son can snag a dowry from the family of a bride that must provide cash or cattle to have him take the daughter off its hands.

What a reporter for *The Hindu* called "the fear of giving birth to female babies" now has technological teeth. Health officials said that many parents still obtain sex ID scans via amniocentesis despite legal pressure on doctors not to provide such information. When one mark on the screen is missing, abortion beckons. Among those not so technologically adept, infanticide is common.

All of that is just a new twist in India's long history of violence. Scholars often refer to the period of the Gupta dynasty in Northern India (4th to 6th century AD) as India's Classical Age, but a whole lot of fighting went on during that golden time. The armies of Samudra Gupta, who became king in about AD 335, defeated the armies of four northern kings in the area around Delhi. Gupta's army fought its way down the east coast and forced kings to pay him homage. Gupta's soldiers "violently uprooted" nine kingdoms in the western half of the Ganges plain, according to an ancient memorial pillar.

Similar battles occurred in each era. The true pacifists of India were Jains, not Hindus, and I climbed one day to Jain caves on rock outcroppings rising five hundred feet above the plain near Madurai, India. The Jains stayed on the rock so they would not hurt plant life, but Hindus fought them. Later, dueling Hindu factions, Shaivites and Vaishnavites, regularly destroyed each other's temples. As V. I. Naipaul (*India: A Wounded Civilization*) wrote, Gandhi from 1919 through 1930 gave "the world a new idea of India," with nonviolence "made to appear an ancient, many-sided Indian truth, an eternal source of Hindu action." But in reality India "was cruel and horribly violent."

That violence is making a comeback in the twenty-first century, as doctrines of Hindutva (Hindu spiritedness) are gaining political ascendancy in much of India.

Hinduunity.org argues that "Gandhi was a downright PACI-FIST, without guts and SCRUPLES. His constant preaching to his fellow Hindus, to be non violent at all times, EVEN IN THE FACE OF AGGRESSION, paralyzed the manhood of India." Today, though, Indians are becoming "Soldiers of Hindutva . . . . Young, strong and fearless groups of Hindus who are willing to die for the cause of Hindutva. The protectors of the faith!"

One night at the eighth-century Valkuntha Perumal temple in the little village of Kancheepuram, I shone a flashlight on some wall sculptures and found the figure of a man undergoing punishment by being impaled on a sharp stake. Later I read Hinduunity.org's further declaration: "Our policy is simple. Don't mess with Hinduism, its followers and our mother land of India or we'll mess with you. Hindu youths need to know the truth like it is. If they don't take a stand now, their children will be going to Mosques and Churches within no time."

Hinduunity.org is not Hinduism. Many Hindus are peaceful and tolerant, but Hinduism is diverse.

Hindu Time Line from AD 800 to the Present

820 AD India's most famous philosopher, Sankara, dies. He has argued that the world is illusion and the cosmic spirit is the sole reality.

850 Era of Manikkavasagar, Shaivite author of the *Tiruvasagam,* a set of fifty-one poems showing how individual souls connect with Siva.

1100 Era of Ramanuja, a bhakti-emphasizing, theistic philosopher, and the foremost opponent of Sankara's system.

1300 Era of Madhva, who believed that god and man were distinct and thus opposed Sankara's monistic system.

1500 Era of Kabir, a Vaishnavite reformer whose songs are still popular.

1528 Muslim conqueror Babur solidifies his control by destroying a temple at Ayodha, Rama's purported birthplace, and erecting a mosque in its place.

1649 Tukaram, a composer famed for his hymns to Krishna, dies.

1796 Over two million worshippers fight for room to bathe in the Ganges at Kumbha Mela in Hardwar. Five thousand Shaivite ascetics die.

1828 Ram Mohan Roy founds a social reform movement that repudiates polytheism, idol worship, the Vedas, karma, reincarnation, and the caste system.

1837 The British suppress Kali-worshipping Thugees, who have taken up an extreme form of Hinduism.

1850 H. H. Wilson produces the first English translation of the Rig Veda.

1875 Russian mystic Madame H. P. Blavatsky founds the Theosophical Society with the goal of bringing aspects of Hinduism and other Eastern religions to the west.

1876 Professor Max Muller begins publication of a fifty-volume Sacred Books of the East series.

1893 Swami Vivekananda evangelizes America for Hinduism at the Chicago world's fair Parliament of the World's Religions.

1913 Poet Rabindranath Tagore receives the Nobel Prize for Literature.

1919 Mahatma Gandhi begins advocating the *satyagraha* (firmness in truth) strategy of pacifistic noncooperation in regard to India's British rulers.

1946 Paramahamsa Yogananda popularizes Hinduism with his *Autobiography of a Yogi*.

1947 India gains independence from Britain, with Pakistan becoming a separate Muslim country and 600,000 dying in riots as 14 million people move back and forth.

1948 A Hindu editor assassinates Gandhi because of Gandhi's efforts to bring about peace between Hindus and Muslims.

1949 India's new constitution officially bans discrimination on the basis of caste and officially eliminates "untouchability."

1967 The Beatles become interested in Transcendental Meditation, and Maharishi Mahesh Yogi becomes famous.

1981 Statistics show that India is home to half of the world's cattle, with eight cows for every ten Indians.

1992 Hindu nationalists demolish the mosque built in Ayodhya in 1548 by Muslim conqueror Babar after he destroyed a Hindu temple on the site.

Chapter Five

Buddhism's Detachment

One of Judaism's appeals is its tight boundary-drawing. One appeal of Hinduism is its apparent flexibility. Buddhism, which has perhaps 350 million adherents worldwide, including one million in the United States, attracts many because it says that all such considerations are irrelevant. The experience of Thomas Kirchner, who grew up Roman Catholic in New Haven, typifies that of American converts: When he and I spoke in Kyoto, Japan, he explained how he became "a doubter enthralled by a doubt-based religion, Zen Buddhism." An undergraduate at Duke in the late 1960s, Kirchner sneered at everything until a visiting lecturer explained Zen as the antifaith faith. Kirchner soon went to Japan and was further attracted by what he heard: "Zen says, 'You doubt? Great. You haven't doubted enough.'"

Zen is just one variety of Buddhism, but the whole religion, judging by the remarks of students entering my Journalism and Religion class, benefits from a superb public image in America: They described Buddhism as "peace, love, and goodness. Very calm. Super chilled out. Centered.

Nonviolent." Kirchner, now with three decades of experience as a Buddhist monk in Kyoto, is no longer excited about orthodox Buddhist activities like monastic retreats (where the "last thing you want to do is meditate"). He is turned off by Buddhist life at Japanese universities, where he "saw people utterly distorting Buddhist spirituality so they could get tenure." But he is still enthralled with the person of Siddhartha Gautama, known as the Buddha (enlightened one), Sakyamuni Buddha (Buddha of the Sakya clan), or Bhagavat (Lord) to his followers.

The Buddha was born near the border of present-day India and Nepal and lived sometime in the fifth and sixth centuries BC (his followers disagree on the dates). The standard story is that Siddhartha's parents were the king and queen of the Sakya Kingdom, one of many Indian principalities. (Others, though, say that the Sakyas had no king but were ruled by a oligarchic council of elders.) According to legend, Siddhartha's mother dreamed the night before his birth that an elephant carrying a lotus flower in its trunk entered her womb through the right side of her body, signifying that the child would be great. Soon after birth the infant Siddhartha is said to have walked seven steps in each of the four directions, while lotus flowers sprouted where his feet touched the earth. The baby is then said to have announced, "No further births have I to endure, for this is my last body. Now shall I destroy and pluck out by the roots the sorrow that is caused by birth and death."

Hindus at that time tried to discern the future of children by various marks on their bodies; Siddhartha's parents gave him that name, "one whose aim is accomplished," because his thirty-two marks indicated that he was a Buddha, an Enlightened One. The story is that Siddhartha lived in great luxury and wealth, with his father King Suddhodana trying so hard to keep him from being upset that when Siddhartha went out for a walk the king employed smiling people to fill the path. The Buddha is later reported to have said of his childhood, "I was delicately nurtured, exceedingly delicately nurtured, delicately nurtured beyond measure. . . . I had three palaces: one for winter, one for summer and one for the rainy season. . . . In the rainy season palace, during the four months of the rains, entertained only by female musicians, I did not come down from the palace."

When he was twenty-nine, though, sheltered Gautama saw a decrepit old man and also "a sick man, suffering and very ill, fallen and weltering in his own excreta." He became especially agitated upon seeing a dead body, but then he saw a wandering monk who was serene in the face of such misery and wanted to be like him. Gautama made the Great Renunciation, "to give up the princely life and become a wandering ascetic," and immediately left his wife and infant son to head south to centers of spiritual discipline. Many dissident gurus were at his disposal, for Gautama lived in a world of religious rebellion against early Hinduism, with Jainists (absolute pacifists), Ajivakas (nihilists), Lokayatas (materialists), and the Samara movement (wandering beggars who renounced the world) all competing for adherents.

Gautama went from teacher to teacher but was unsatisfied and then almost starved himself over the next six years.

Later he recalled that "all my limbs became like some withered creepers with knotted joints . . . the skin of my belly came to be cleaving to by back-bone." He became so weak that he saw he could not gain enlightenment that way and started taking care of himself. Then came a night when he sat at the base of a tree and had a breakthrough: he later wrote that "his mind was emancipated . . . Ignorance was dispelled, science (knowledge) arose; darkness was dispelled, light arose."

Gautama had not come to understand gravity while sitting under a tree, as Isaac Newton is said to have done, but something even more grave: that life is suffering. He learned of his former existences, gained power to see the deaths and rebirths of others, and realized the Four Noble Truths: Life is suffering; suffering is caused by our attachments to the world and people around us; we can end suffering by developing nonattachment; and we can advance our consciousness by acting and thinking in specific ways.

The Buddha spent the next forty-five years of his life traveling on foot through Northern India and preaching about doing everything in moderation, so that neither fleshly delights nor their utter absence would leave people thinking about material rather than spiritual things. He ate meat—that may have been expedience, because beggars could not be choosers—and apparently died after eating contaminated mushrooms or pork. Shortly before his death, when asked who would be the post-Gautama authority concerning matters of doctrine, he replied that each individual's sense of dharma should rule. Buddhism thus became more a general philosophy, onto which additions can readily be grafted, than a fixed doctrine.

In essence Gautama developed a positivist faith that we can turn ourselves into wise beings without needing a God who probably does not exist. Early Hinduism was filled with sacrifices and ritual; early Buddhism stripped away glitz and emphasized mind control through meditation. Such a faith has appealed to hundreds of millions, including in the U.S. members of "the beat generation" during the 1950s. In recent years Hollywood stars like Richard Gere and Sharon Stone, as well as Bible haters like Oliver Stone, have signed up; Mr. Stone complained that "Christ was all about pain and suffering," and said Buddhism helped him "get out from under the monstrously oppressive God the Father."

It's hard, though, to know what in Buddhist teaching authentically came from the Buddha. He had many disciples and a large following by the time of his death in his early eighties, but his words were not written down until about 250 years after his death. Then priests wrote down more and more: The scriptures of one of the two main divisions of Buddhism, Theravada, are eleven times longer than the Bible. The scriptures of the other main division, Mahayana, are more numerous still, encompassing more than five thousand volumes. (A third, Tibetan division, Vajrayana, has many scriptures as well.)

This means that no one can carry all of Buddhist scripture to temple worship as many Christians carry the Bible to church. Sects typically emphasize favorite *sutras* (writings) and forget about others. Moreover, various Buddhist leaders quarrel about even the core teachings of their faith. Individual teachers have great latitude to shape their particular kind of Buddhism. Disciples tend to cluster around particular teachers, and Buddhist leaders sometimes become heated in criticizing other Buddhists.

But with all the battles, the appeal of Buddhism is strong for those who have tasted the world's pleasures and found them wanting. Buddhism, born and developed in a culture of great poverty and suffering, emphasizes the greed, hatred, and ignorance that naturally envelop us. It then loads that realistic sense of human nature onto a Hindu truck that runs on karmic transmigration, the doctrine that after death the essence of a person is reborn in another body.

To go through this quickly, people can be reborn into six realms: The top three are gods, titans, and humans, and the bottom three are ghosts, animals, and hell. Rebirth depends on actions in this life and past ones: Negative emotions lead to negative actions which lead to negative karma which can result in rebirth as a fish, dog, or cockroach. The cycle can continue for eternity and ends only when a person attains *nirvana,* the extinction of individuality and entrance into the cosmic all. (Buddhism denies the existence of self as an object that is distinct from other selves.)

Conventional Buddhists say the cycle takes at least seven lives but might take millions. In the classic Buddhist understanding, individuals progress by dropping all worldly attachments and emphasizing extensive meditation, strenuous physical exercises, and other means of turning off our egos. Buddhism wins support on those grounds from people tired of being consumed by consumerism, but it's important to note that Buddhists condemn not only attachments to houses and cars: They also say they have foolish attachment to their own lives and to others. The Buddha himself named his son Rahula, which means "obstacle," and then abandoned his wife and son to seek enlightenment.

Two Buddhist parables illustrate the sweeping nature of the nonattachment principle. One concerns a man, fleeing a tiger, who comes to the edge of a cliff, finds a vine, and climbs down it. When almost down he discovers that a second tiger awaits him at the bottom, while mice chew the vine above him. Instead of trying to concoct a means of escape, he notices a wild strawberry growing on the face of the cliff and eats it. Then the vine breaks, and the tiger gobbles up the man. End of story. Non-Buddhists might see this tale as one of horror or might wonder why the man didn't desperately try to distract the tiger by tossing the strawberry to him. But the primary point is that as strawberry is to man, so man is to tiger: we should not be attached to our own lives. Furthermore, we are all part of the whole, and if we have the right understanding we will not fear death because we cannot die.

The second Buddhist story concerns a monk, Katayana, who walked through a forest, saw a man, a woman, and a baby joyfully eating lunch, and burst out laughing at the deluded family values of the diners. Katayana told his disciples, "They're eating a fish that they caught from the lake. That fish was the grandfather in a former life. The dog who is now barking and begging for the fish was the grandmother.

The baby the mother is holding to her breast was the husband's enemy, a man he had killed for assaulting his wife." At the core of Buddhism is a sense that our attachments are foolish and that if we get rid of them we will control our emotions and avoid creating additional suffering for us in this life and future ones.

Some Buddhist handbooks teach the principle of nonattachment (to anyone as well as to anything) by recounting the life of the Buddha himself: He "renounced his family, wealth, and power and fled to the mountains to meditate upon the way of truth." They stress that the way to beat attachment is through meditation. For example, a strong attachment to a girlfriend's appearance can be beaten by looking deeper into her body, into what it's made of. Buddhists are to look past the skin and visualize the veins, organs, bacteria, and so on. Similarly, a Thai abbot stated, "Lust should be balanced by contemplation of loathsomeness. . . . Examine the body as a corpse and see the process of decay or think of the parts of the body such as the lungs, spleen, fat, feces, and so forth."

That animosity toward the body is frequent in Buddhism. One popular Web page asks, "What is the body really? What more is it than a skin bag filled with bones, flesh, disgusting organs, and fluids?" That view doesn't note that we are fearfully and wonderfully made, but much of Buddhism misses trees and emphasizes gloom about the forest. One of Christianity's most famous catechism answers is Westminster No. 1, which notes that "man's chief purpose is to glorify God and enjoy Him forever." The Buddha's "noble truths" have nothing about accentuating that positive; they are about suffering and how to eliminate the negative.

That dislike for our material bodies is coupled with a disbelief in a sovereign God or gods. Some Buddhists posit the existence of a spirit world with gods in the heavens, but gods are not supreme: Their hero is the Buddha, the man who became fully enlightened and told his followers to go and do likewise. Buddhists are not supposed to spend their time contemplating creation, since all matter is illusion or manifestation of the Ultimate Reality. Their standard goal is to concentrate on individual enlightenment and to break out of the cycle of transmigration that Buddhists call *samsara,* or "endless wandering."

Those who are attached to someone or something are to reflect on the impermanence of whatever we love. If a Buddhist is attached to a bell, he is to remember all the things that could go wrong with it: It could lose its sound, it could crack, it could be dropped and broken, and so on. Non-attachment demands a distancing even from love for ideas. As one Buddhist textbook explains, the goal is "to root out each and every point of attachment until there is not even a speck of dust left for the mind to grasp. This means that not only such coarse forms of attachment as the passions and desires must be left behind, but also the more subtle threads of intellectual attachment." Theoretically, that should include attachment even to Buddhist ideas.

The Noble Eightfold Path apparently laid out by Buddha as a way to eliminate suffering includes Right Speech (telling the truth in love), Right Action (saying no to wrong behavior such as killing, stealing, or adultery), Right Livelihood (saying no to work that causes harm to others), and Right Mindfulness (being aware of surroundings). Other aspects suggest an escape from reason: Right Meditation (developing deep mental calm through techniques that concentrate the mind), Right View (accepting the Buddhist worldview), Right Resolve (committing to total attitude adjustment), and Right Effort (the activities designed to bring about personality change).

Since strict constructionist Buddhism does not hold that people need to be changed by God, it is full of tips on the effort needed to change themselves. Breathing exercises can settle the mind—I've seen them work during the delivery of three of my children—and that's where Buddhists often begin. Many claim this can lead to great things: "Feel the air coming in and going out. Visualize the air as a sort of bluish incense smoke. You are creating a diversion, turning the attraction or attention of your mind to something other than" attachment to life—such as constructing in your mind a bridge.

Many would-be Buddhists find such techniques do not work, but Buddhist leaders emphasize perseverance: "If doing it once doesn't work, you can do it 21 times. You can build 21 bridges. And if you have all the time in the world, build 100 bridges." Serious Buddhists realize they must build thousands of bridges and may make time by dropping out of other activities. The pursuit of tranquility can become agitated because the individual's destiny is entirely his own responsibility.

If the individual does stabilize his emotions through such breathing exercises, analytical meditation can begin: Each person in a sense argues himself into believing that the ego is the enemy. Such meditation for conventional Buddhists is parallel to Bible reading for Jews and Christians, except that the process in Buddhism is internal, while for Bible readers it involves having an external message act upon the individual. Many Buddhists turn inward by repeating mantras—combinations of sounds and words—that they believe raise good vibrations within a person and open up his deeper consciousness. They say that reciting the same chants day after day produces not boredom but wholesome karma.

This emphasis on the internal can appeal to those tired of liberal and Marxist clichés about the goodness of man and his corruption by the external environment. Many people have enough self-consciousness to realize that humans are not good by nature; a Tibetan Buddhist text such as *Good Life, Good Death* by Rimpoche Gehlek, a "reincarnated lama," resonates with that understanding. Gehlek states, "The true enemy is inside. The maker of trouble, the source of all our suffering, the destroyer of our virtue is inside. It is Ego. . . . So your boss is not responsible for your hurt pride, your parents did not create your rage. We blame conditions while the problem and the cause of our problem is inside."

The inward turning of Buddhism is revealed in the question-and-answer sessions on some Web sites, including this one provided by Ajahn Chah, a monk in Ubon Rajathani in northeastern Thailand: "Q: Is it advisable to read a lot or study the scriptures as a part of practice? A: You don't need to bother with books. Watch your own mind. Examine to see how feelings come and go, how thoughts come and go. Don't be attached to anything. Q: A lot of times it seems that many monks here are not practicing. They look sloppy or unmindful. This disturbs me. A: You will not discover wisdom watching others."

The Eightfold Path can readily appeal to those who see that changing external environments doesn't work and then decide to concentrate on the internal. The Buddhist equivalent of original sin is the realization that anger gives us temporary satisfaction. Gehlek put it well: "When we scream at someone we may be embarrassed later but we enjoy it at the time. . . . Later you might regret it, but regret is not hooking you, it's satisfaction that's hooking you. If satisfaction weren't part of it, you wouldn't get hooked into it again and again. . . . And when you let anger go unchecked, anger comes much more often. . . . Yelling, screaming, shouting and tantrums become a habit. This can make you feel as though you've gained the upper hand."

The secret to happiness for individuals and the world is for people to control their egos. The ego is selfish, but the ego is not the person; the individual can look at the ego from the outside and, through his own power, control it. As Gehlek notes, "If you don't watch your mind it will be like letting a monkey into a museum without a guard. The monkey will take a big brush and paint over all the paintings. With jealousy he'll paint them green, with anger he'll paint them red, with attachment blue—he'll put paint all over. So it's time for us to catch that monkey." Many Buddhists believe they can catch the monkey by themselves or with the help of one trainer.

Because much of Buddhism is internally directed, Buddhists tend to be agnostic concerning the basic nature of existence. Many Buddhists do not believe in any kind of god or gods. Some hold that there is a spirit world with gods in the heavens, but gods are not supreme and are subject to rebirth, while only humans have the potential to attain Enlightenment and reach nirvana. The hero of Buddhism is the Buddha, "the Awakened One," who is revered above all not as a god but as the model of a fully enlightened person. Some Buddhists believe that the historic Buddha, the person Siddartha Gautama, was an emanation of a higher power; individual teachers have great latitude to shape their particular understanding of who the Buddha was.

Buddhists also tend to be agnostic about how the world began. Creation is something many Buddhists spend little time thinking about because all matter in one sense is illusion, and origin issues are irrelevant to the task of Enlightenment. Some Buddhists stipulate that the universe has many levels, including four underworlds and twenty-one heavenly realms. But who cares? People need to rid themselves of self-consciousness by dropping all worldly cravings and desires as wisdom and meditation replace overindulgence and the acquisition of worldly possessions. Leading a virtuous life takes a person part way to Nirvana, but wisdom, a deep understanding of man's situation, is needed for the rest of the journey.

Most Buddhist leaders teach that it is within our own power to live rightly: we do not need to be changed by god (no such being exists, according to many Buddhists). Wisdom begins with recognition that we are the Buddhist equivalent of sinners: we have anger and jealousy that leads to expressions of hatred. We have attachments to people or things that we place above our pursuit of Nirvana.

Any person can potentially achieve Buddhahood, transcending personality and becoming one with the impersonal Ultimate Reality, which is Infinite Bliss (Nirvana). We need to look at negative emotions and stop denying them. We must resolve to fix problems by recognizing that we control our own lives and are able to create positive karma. At the least we can control our emotional habits and cease our habits of anger and attachment that create additional suffering for us in this life and the next one.

Traditional Buddhists suggest that the best way to transform an outlook from narrow and selfish to balanced and altruistic is to become a monk and lead a life of wandering, poverty, begging, and sexual abstinence. A Buddhist monk was allowed to own three robes and one belt, along with an alms bowl, a razor, a needle, and a water strainer used to filter insects from the drinking water. The standards on poverty, begging, and sexual abstinence have been loosened in recent years among many monks. Some have given up the nomadic life and settled in monasteries, which often over time develop a hierarchical structure.

Buddhists do not pray as Jews, Christians, or Muslims pray because they turn their devotional meditations inward rather than outward. When I visited one Buddhist meditation center, I was told, "Take your glasses off." The instructor said I could not learn much by reading; I had to look within. Some Buddhists believe they can benefit others by radiating love to all life forms and can even share their merit so that their karmic force helps others. Overall, though, Buddhist morality is based not so much on how an action affects others as on how it affects an individual's personality.

One practical application of this is the desire to give money to, say, homeless men even if they will quickly use it to purchase drugs or alcohol: the emphasis is on how almsgiving affects the giver, not the recipient. Actions inspired by greed, hatred, and delusion are bad, but those motivated by nonattachment, benevolence, and understanding are good. We cannot gain a true understanding of the world as illusion, and thereby move toward Nirvana, as long as we are attached to anything, including our own lives.

Attachment to individuals, which includes loving them, means embracing a lie, for as the Buddha taught, "I have killed all of you before. I was chopped up by all of you in previous lives. We have all killed each other as enemies. So why should we be attached to each other?" Seemingly altruistic attachment is really egotistical because it means we are trying to build pleasant lives for ourselves instead of realizing that all is suffering.

A detached state of mind is important for the young, as a way of turning desire into patience. It becomes especially crucial for the old, as pressures of sickness and impending death make it harder to believe that the external is not real.

Buddhists typically tell the dying that "your state of mind at the time you draw your last breath is crucial, for upon this hinges your following rebirth. Only a disciplined or spiritually prepared mind can hope to resist the pull of karmic forces—i.e., old patterns of craving and clinging—as the final energies are slipping away so that a higher level of rebirth, and even enlightenment itself, may be attained."

Death is often a high-pressure situation, like the seventh game of a World Series, because what happens in a few seconds can have an effect that lasts a lifetime (or, given reincarnation, many lifetimes). Gehlek advises, "No matter what happens during the dying process, or what you go through, don't forget to remain in a positive frame of mind of love and compassion. Don't let pain or worry cloud your concentration." Visualize good things because "visualizing this way can make your future life better."

Tibetan Buddhists have the process of dying worked out in terms of earth, water, fire, and air—nature's building blocks in both Buddhist and ancient Greek thought—leaving the body one after the other. Here's Gehlek's recommendation: "When you see the signs of the elements dissolving— water, smoke, red sparks, flickering candlelight—then you know that the body is about to separate from the mind. Soon you'll see a whitish light, then a reddish haze, then darkness. Right at that moment is when you have a chance to work with your pure nature to become enlightened." Painkilling drugs that impair the clarity of consciousness are definitely out. Weeping relatives or last words about wills are also an encumbrance. Some Buddhists advise gazing at a favorite picture of the Buddha and chanting poems as long as speech remains.

Those who have not done any spiritual exercises and have led selfish lives may find themselves in a miserable condition. Zen master Ekaku said in the 1700s:

> When these people die, at first they do not have
> a proper body, and it is as if they had entered into
> a deep sleep. But after a while their "root-nature"
> becomes fixed, and then they open their eyes and
> find that they have fallen into the city of darkness.
> . . . They begin to notice the mountains of "After-
> Death" and the valley of the three hells. Then they
> have to grope their way for ten or twenty miles till
> they come out onto a broad limitless plain, where
> there is no sun or moon but only great conflagra-
> tions burning with the flames flaring up to the sky.
> Here they see sinners crowded together weeping
> bitterly. And the newcomers think, "Alas, have we
> sunk down into this dreadful place? Oh, if only we
> had known about this . . . but we thought all the
> talk about this sort of thing was the idle talk of
> men of false views."

Petas, sometimes referred to as "hungry ghosts," live in the lowest heavenly world but, because of their previous deeds, are unable to enjoy its pleasures. They generally can't even drink the water of the river Ganges, for it turns to blood when they scoop it up in their hands. The good news is that at some point the penalty for the deed that brought a peta to that state is paid up. At that point, once the peta receives an offering from a still living human relative, his distress disappears and he can enjoy the pleasures around him.

The human gati is one of the better places to be, except that even those at the top need to remember that their situation is impermanent. The Buddha frequently pointed out that of those who die in the human and heavenly gatis, few regain such a birth again. Most are born in the lower three gatis. One problem is that those in the three lower gatis have a hard time generating good karma that might allow them to attain a better rebirth when their period there comes to an end. That's bad news, because it's easy to get stuck there.

In other ways as well, those who go deeper into Buddhism find complications in its simple nonattachment principles. Buddhist monks have been arguing for a long time about whether only one way to nonattachment exists or whether multiple paths are possible. Early Buddhism was for monks only; that's what most of the participants decided at the First Buddhist Council, perhaps held soon after the death of Gautama. The classic goal was to achieve Nirvana through ascetic self-effort based on monastic vows. Early Buddhists were to detach themselves from sensual and impure desires and thoughts and replace those with a meditative state of concentration and joy, but that's just the beginning. The goal was to lose every emotion and become indifferent to everything, moving beyond any sense of satisfaction, pain, or serenity.

That appealed to some intellectuals, but Buddhism's expansion two thousand years ago ran into a wall. Many people did not want nonattachment if it meant a farewell to love. Even those who made spiritual progress were supposed to realize that how far they could go toward Nirvana would depend on what had transpired in previous lives. In practice, even Buddhist monks often found they made little progress toward eliminating desire. Ordinary people could make even less. Besides, even a person who grasped Buddhist truth would still need seven rebirths—and then what? This faith had limited appeal.

Around AD 100 some Buddhists stemmed their religion's downslide with a theological innovation. They came up with the concept of bodhisattvas, enlightened beings who could have attained Nirvana but purposefully chose to put it off in order to help others reach Nirvana far more quickly than they otherwise would. The origin of the belief that faith in a self-sacrificing bodhisattva is essential, is lost in the mists of time, but its emergence shortly after Christianity arrived in India is probably not coincidental.

The new Buddhism, called *Mahayana* ("great way"), developed many variants over the years. For example, some Japanese Mahayana Buddhists gravitated to *zazen* (meditation), developed in the twelfth and thirteenth centuries by teachers who had studied in India and China. Zen Buddhists taught that the faithful should pay no attention to rational thought processes. They came up with famous Zen questions—What is the sound of one hand clapping?—designed to force thinkers to conclude that rational thought is inadequate and should be abandoned. (The most famous Christian medieval question—How many angels can dance on the head of a pin?—was designed to produce the opposite of mysticism. Students were expected to think through the problem and conclude that an infinite number could, since angels are incorporeal spirits.)

Today perhaps 30 percent of Buddhists worldwide stick with the original form, Theravada Buddhism (sometimes disparagingly referred to as Hinayana, "little way"). Theravadas point out Mahayana contradictions: in a karmic system grace should play no part and individual "merit" is all, so does it make sense to believe in bodhisattvas who can give great amounts of their accumulated merit to others who can then move up? Theravadas still try to achieve Nirvana through ascetic self-effort based on monastic vows that both men and women can take. Enlightenment begins with clear memory, the exact investigation of things, and requires achievement of the four sublime states: sympathy, tranquility, impartiality, and a disposition for concentration. Ritual chanting and worship of relics of a Buddha or things made by a Buddha are said to help in this process.

Theravadas try to detach themselves from all material attachments and replace those with a state of concentration and joy—but that's just the beginning. The goal is to lose every emotion and become indifferent to everything, moving beyond any sense of satisfaction, pain, or serenity, so that the mediator is not inclined to either a good or bad state of mind. Without that single-mindedness those who meditate may find joy in their particular living situation, but the Buddhist truth to be grasped is that "all reality is without self and impermanent and is filled with suffering."

Even though an individual may see much progress in discarding emotions, how far he can go toward Nirvana depends on previous lives. A person who has grasped Buddhist truth and gained some sense of what Nirvana is will experience no more than seven rebirths. A person further along may need only one additional rebirth. Truly advanced practitioners may gain complete liberation from the bonds of craving and thus be Nirvana eligible. Theravada Buddhists view Buddha as a man and not a bodhisattva. They deny the existence of other Buddhas and insist that Enlightenment only comes through individual effort.

Meanwhile, Mahayana Buddhism has maintained its social orientation. Adherents still are to strive to have the capacity to become Buddhas but are to forego immediate entry into Nirvana so they can become bodhisattvas and help others by transferring their extra karmic merit to those they wish. One popular Mahayana denomination, called Pure Land (*jodo* in Japanese) tells the story of a monk, Dharmakara, who promised to create a Pure Land paradise in the west if he became a Buddha. He succeeded, so in this Pure Land evil does not exist, and people can have whatever they want. Those with faith in this Buddha get to go after death to the Pure Land where conditions for liberation are excellent and the reincarnation process can be shortened.

Various Buddhist cults have developed mantras that, when repeated thousands of times, will purportedly help the mind to overcome any surroundings. One school of thought, for example, teaches that constant invocation of the name Amitabha Buddha will transport the meditator to the Pure

Land. Critics pointed out flaws in the Mahayana approach, noting that bodhisattvas are only imagined saviors, not a real person like Jesus who lived at a specific time. Others noted that the goal of bodhisattvas is to help people attain Nirvana faster, but Nirvana—the extinction of personality—is not necessarily a destination with wide appeal.

Nevertheless, Mahayana is the dominant form of Buddhism in Japan and in most of the rest of the world, and the Pure Land approach has become the most popular denomination. Thervada Buddhism is dominant only in Southeast Asia. Buddhism arrived in the United States in the early nineteenth century along with Chinese and Japanese immigrants and became popular, in its Zen variety, among members of the American cultural left during the 1950s and 1960s.

Today racial and cultural divides separate American Buddhists. Asian-American Buddhists tend to see temples as important religious and cultural centers, but European-descent Buddhists tend to emphasize meditation, often seeing Buddhism as a set of concepts to mix and match with other beliefs. In addition, meditative techniques associated with Buddhism and physical exercises such as yoga are popular with many who do not dip more than a toe into the ocean of Buddhist theology.

Also picking up some support in the U.S. is Vajrayana Buddhism, the "diamond way" developed in Tibet, with its belief that Nirvana is achieved only when people combine passivity with *karuna* (active compassion). The enlightened are to realize that the two elements are one. Tibetan

Buddhism is also gaining attention through the ministrations of its leader, the Dalai Lama, and several Hollywood stars.

Buddhism Glossary

Amitabha Buddha The bodhisattva said to have used his merit to establish the Pure Land in the west, which those with faith in him can enter.

Anatman The concept that no eternal soul exists and that each individual instead is made up of five skandas that lose their bonding power at death.

Arhat A person who has attained Nirvana.

Bhikkhu Buddhist monk.

Bodhisattva A person who has attained Enlightenment but delayed Nirvana so as to help those who are suffering.

Buddha Literally, "awakened one": a person who has been released from the world of cyclic existence (samsara) and has attained liberation from desire, craving, and attachment.

Dalai Lama Tibetan leader said by his devotees to be a reincarnation of the bodhisattva of compassion.

Dharma The cosmic law underlying all existence and teachings about it.

Dukkha Suffering, which according to the Buddha is the essence of life.

Five Precepts The minimum set of moral rules for Buddhism, with theft, killing, lying, drinking alcohol, and adultery (for monks, all sexual activity) banned.

Four Noble Truths The Buddha's basic statement: all is dukkha, dukkha results from desire, elimination of desire leads to elimination of suffering, and the Noble Eight-fold Path is the highway to personal progress.

Hinayana Buddhism "The Little Way," a derogatory term for Theravada Buddhism used by Mahayana ("Great Way") Buddhists.

Impermanence One of the reasons for suffering: all people and things decay and die.

Karma Literally, "action"; the universal law of cause and effect that governs rebirth and the world of *samsara*. The sum of actions in a life determines the high or low place of rebirth.

Koan A puzzle in Zen Buddhism that can be solved only by instant insight, not by reason or study.

Mahayana Buddhism The most popular form of Buddhism, with an emphasis on bodhisattvas rather than arhats and on how individuals can escape samsara without going through countless lives.

Maitreya The jovial Buddha, expected to come in the future, who is often depicted with a smile on his face and a big belly.

Mandala A work of art, often a painting or tapestry, that emphasizes circles as a symbol of eternal continuity and often becomes an object of worship.

Nirvana Literally "extinction, blowing out"; the goal of spiritual practice in Buddhism; liberation from the cycle of rebirth and suffering, with the end of suffering coming through the extinction of personality and union with Ultimate Reality.

Noble Eightfold Path The way to reach Enlightenment by having "Right Views, Right Intent, Right Speech, Right

Conduct, Right Livelihood, Right Effort, Right Mindfulness, and Right Concentration."

Puja An act of devotion or worship.

Pure Land Buddhism The form of Mahayana Buddhism that gives hope to people far from enlightenment and apparently doomed to remain in samsara: they can call on Amitabha Buddha and be taken when they die to a paradise in the west.

Rinpoche "Greatly precious" in Tibetan Buddhism, a term applied to spiritual masters.

Sakymuni Title given to the Buddha, meaning "wise one of the Sakya tribe."

Samadhi Meditation in which the mind concentrates on a single object and becomes so calm that the distinction between the object and the person thinking about it seems to disappear.

Samsara The cycle of birth, death, and rebirth that leaves all people in a world of suffering.

Sangha Term for the Buddhist monastic community that now has come to include the entire community of Buddhist practitioners.

Satori Enlightenment.

Skandas The five elements of a person (body, feelings, perceptions, habits, and consciousness) that purportedly come together at birth and separate at death.

Stupa A temple in which relics of the Buddha are kept.

Theravada Buddhism This earliest form of Buddhism, literally "the path of the Elders," emphasizes the need of the individual to attain enlightenment through meditation so as to become an arhat and then attain Nirvana.

The Three Jewels Buddha, Sangha, and Dharma: awakened person, community, cosmic law.

Tripitaka Three baskets that contain the three main sacred writings of Buddhism: teachings of the Buddha, teachings of the sangha, and special teachings.

Vajrayana "Diamond Way" Buddhism, practiced largely in Tibet, which claims to teach a person to use all of his powers so as to reach Nirvana in one lifetime.

Zen Buddhism A branch of Mahayana Buddhism that developed in China and Japan and is now popular in Europe and the United States. Zen Buddhists emphasize meditation and believe that reality is beyond language or logic.

Chapter Six

The Japanese Experience

Ask most American students about Buddhism and the response, if there is any at all, is likely to be either abstract ("an Asian religion") or celebrity driven ("Dalai Lama? Richard Gere?"). But when I traveled to Japan, the country that has the most Buddhists, Buddhism changed for me from a strange religion with millions of adherents to one interwoven with the lives of particular faces in the crowd such as Yamamoto Maya, Takagi Kinho, Honda Yoshinari, and Junko Blockson.

Yamamoto Maya (I am following Japanese style by placing family names first) is a Japanese woman in her forties with a mottled face, freckles, and some bruising under one eye. She smiles but seems sad, and when she talks, she is intense, as befits a person who has had a hard life. Her parents divorced when she was young and neither wanted to take care of her. She was the fifth and youngest child, with grown-up brothers and sisters who also abandoned her. She was sent around to the homes of various relatives as half maid, half slave.

As Maya grew older, she tried to have herself committed to an orphanage, but those who mistreated her would not allow an action that would bring public shame to the family that was acting shamefully. Finally she married, only to have her husband beat her, break her bones and teeth, and put her in the hospital. She and her husband had one child, but that did not improve their marriage. A decade ago, with her son a toddler, she began coming to a Buddhist temple on Mount Koya-san, a beautiful hill in central Japan about a two-hour drive from the crowded streets of Osaka.

I saw some of what Mrs. Yamamoto did at the temple to find relief from her pain. At 10:20 on a cool Saturday evening, she waited on steps leading down to a cold river, her hands clasped before her. It was dark, with incense burning so that for those more than ten yards away smell had to replace sight. She wore a white robe, indicating purity, and threw handfuls of salt into the water, as another purifying gesture. She began chanting the names of Buddha, fast, loud, without seemingly stopping for breath. She let out an animal-sounding scream ("VEE-AYE"), entered the water, and stood chanting for ten minutes. She later said that during that time she felt Buddha enter her body.

Yamamoto Maya's sad history of suffering provides exactly the type of background that would lead a person to believe that life is suffering, and to search for an escape, any escape. Seeking Nirvana means seeking the elimination of individuality, but it also means attainment of a state where there will be no more pain, an appealing prospect to Mrs. Yamamoto. Not been taught to pray to a personal god, she has absorbed teaching that the Law of Buddhahood is the law of an impersonal universe. Like it or not, that's the way it is. Nonattachment is better than the attachments of family and marriage that betrayed her.

I also think of Takagi Kinho, twenty-two, who comes from a family of priests and wants to carry on the tradition. To do so he must serve an apprenticeship, and when we met, he was finishing his third year of serving on Mount Koya-san by getting up each morning at five, often after only three hours sleep. He was also going through *kugyo,* literally "hard practice," which consists of ascetic austerities such as sitting with his legs tucked under himself for three to four hours or holding a book of sutras at arm's length for three to four hours. The only food he received during his initial year of training was rice and a little tofu, so he had lost twenty pounds; a beefy fellow trainee lost eighty-eight pounds and, Takagi said, "looked like an African refugee at the end."

Takagi reported that he did not drop out as many did, but "at the end of the first year, I couldn't stop crying." He was resigned to the practice—"To become a priest, you have to do it"—and he laughingly reported some of the humorous highlights: Students have to shave their heads every two days, and "when I first did it, blood came out all over." He was skeptical, though, about the spiritual benefits he had derived from *kugyo,* hard practice. "I don't buy the idea that I will reach *satori,*" the state of illumination, Takagi said. The belief is that you call on a Buddha so many times that you change places with him. "I've called many times and it hasn't happened. But something *shimpi*—spiritually mysterious—is going on here."

When we spoke, Takagi Kinho was planning to leave Mount Koya-san and learn about life in the cities. Students of Buddhism note that the Buddha died at age eighty, lying down, and that his horizontal position contrasts to Christ's painful verticality. Christ is most often depicted in his suffering on the cross, while statues of the Buddha most commonly show him sitting in tranquil meditation. But tranquility is not what Takagi in his early twenties is looking for: he is used to sacrifice and wants to live within the material world but not be attached to it.

The evidence of hard practice was everywhere around me at the temples where I met Yamamoto Maya and Takagi Kinho. Tatami mats at the training center display marks made by the eighty priest apprentices who regularly prostrate themselves. The cemetery includes some priests who died from fasting. They are highly honored, and their *kugyo* certainly showed some courage. And yet why couldn't they see that a person might exhibit a better *kugyo* by giving up bathing in freezing water and instead giving a child a bath? A better *kugyo* is binding up a patient's wounds or working hard to develop a drug that saves lives. Otherwise, religion becomes the opiate of the monks.

Another priest I met, Honda Yoshinari, was born in Hiroshima in 1943, and at age two had to help dispose of atom-bomb-blasted bodies. He is now the priest at a small temple that sits amid the hubbub of Yao, an Osaka exurb that is one of Japan's fastest growing cities. Wearing a black robe and white socks, he padded around on short red carpet during the traditional sutra-chanting service every morning at six or seven, but he kept a blackboard and folding chairs to use during "evangelizing" services that include piano and congregational singing. He cares about those who come to his temple and is clearly attached to his wife and four children, whose names represent what he believes is important: Aya (art/beauty), Makoto (philosophy), Hijiri (religion), and Takumi (morality).

Ironically, Hiroshima may have been the curtain falling on a tragedy partly plotted through doctrines of nonattachment. Although many Americans equate Buddhism with the search for serenity, two books by Methodist-turned-Buddhist Brian Victoria show that Zen Buddhist priests before and during World War II taught Japan's military leaders to be serene about killing others and, if necessary, themselves. As samurai warriors in previous centuries had found Zen's mind control useful in developing combat consciousness, so kamikaze pilots visited Zen monasteries for spiritual preparation before their last flights.

Buddhism also has its parallels to the teaching by some Muslim clerics that dying in the process of killing enemies guarantees passage to paradise. Some Zen priests during World War II told prospective kamikaze attackers that they would gain improved karma for the next life and in a deeper sense would lose nothing since life is unreal and there is really no difference between life and death. Victoria shows that D. T. Suzuki, who taught at Columbia University in the 1950s and became the prime spreader in America of Zen's mystique, stated in 1938 that Zen's "ascetic tendency" helped the Japanese soldier to learn "that to go straight forward and crush the enemy is all that is necessary for him."

Victoria also shows that Hakuun Yasutani, who helped in the 1960s to make Zen popular in the United States, was a major militarist before and during World War II and even wrote in 1943 a book expressing hatred of "the scheming Jews." Stung by such evidence, leaders of Myoshin-ji—the headquarters temple for one major Zen sect—issued shortly after 9/11 an apology noting that "in the past our nation, under the banner of Holy War, initiated a conflict that led to great suffering." Myoshin-ji noted specifically that its members "conducted fundraising drives to purchase military aircraft."

Other Buddhist groups besides the Zen sects supported Japan's aggression and looked to historical warrant for it, and there was plenty. Buddhism first became Japan's established religion fourteen hundred years ago under the aggressive leadership of Shotoku. Buddhists later made an armed camp of their center of power on Mt. Hiei, which overlooks Kyoto, Japan's capital from 794 to 1868. Enryaku-ji, the mountain's first temple, went up in 788, and Buddhists built three thousand more temples on the mountain over the next seven hundred years. Buddhists in the tenth century began basing there an army of many thousands that became known for overthrowing emperors at will. Nine hundred years ago Emperor Shirakawa listed the "three things which I cannot bring under obedience: dice, the waters of a rushing river, and the priests on Mt. Hiei." The Enryaku-ji Buddhists burned down temples of competing sects and even destroyed one temple, Midera, nine times over a 250-year period. One historian of Kyoto, Gouverneur Mosher, noted that "Buddhism did not retard war but rather promoted it."

Other tough Buddhist sects also emphasized anger. One learned Buddhist monk of the thirteenth century, Nichiren, argued that Gautama Buddha as he aged had gradually revealed more and more of the true way to live, which meant that the Buddha's final opus, the Lotus Sutra, was the Buddha's only true, inerrant revelation. He soon developed a Buddhist sect that had its adherents repeat all day long the mystic phrase "Namu Myoho Renge Kyo," which means "Hail to the Lotus Sutra." If people all over Japan would only do that, Nichiren proclaimed, Japan would become a wonderful land in which people could more readily ascend spiritually.

Thus, for Nichiren, politics was next to godliness and crucial for the success of Nichiren's mission: If Nichiren adherents could gain power and command all Japanese to recite the Lotus Sutra, everything would change. Nichiren's anger only intensified as he suffered persecution and then exile for eleven years to a remote island. He attracted those dismayed by Buddhist monks who averted their eyes from problems that could break into their meditative day. Nichiren did not weep as Jesus did when confronted by the death of a friend; instead, when an epidemic occurred, Nichiren raged at government officials, claiming that their bad karma (as well as the misdeeds of other Buddhists) caused the deaths.

The Religions Next Door

Soon entire villages filled with anger adhered to Nichiren ideas and sometimes battled other Buddhist sects.

Buddhist armies fought in the Onin War, which began in 1467 with a dispute about who would be Shogun, the military strongman of Japan. Two armies of about 100,000 men each fought for ten years with Kyoto as the battleground, and the city was destroyed. Disasters over succeeding decades led to more civil wars that culminated in 1536 with the destruction of the Nichiren sect in Kyoto by the Mount Hiei Tendai army, which burned twenty-one temples and killed thousands of priests. But in 1571 the armies of Japanese strongman Oda Nobunaga assaulted the Mount Hiei temples and burned all three thousand, killing thousands of Tendai defenders.

Buddhist leaders were ruthless in suppressing the Christian upsurge of the late sixteenth century that followed the opening of trade with Europe. Beginning on January 3, 1597, six Franciscan friars in Osaka and Kyoto, along with twenty Japanese adherents, had to walk—often through snow—450 miles to Nagasaki, the harbor town on the island of Kyushu that had become a key port for Europeans and the epicenter of Christian growth. The twenty-six were crucified, tied to crosses; they were stabbed to death by a soldier with a javelin on Nishizaka Hill in Nagasaki on February 5.

Government officials, working with Buddhist leaders, persecuted up to 280,000 Christians for their beliefs between 1614 and 1635 and killed about three thousand; for example, on September 10, 1622, officials beheaded thirty converts and burned at the stake twenty-five others, including nine foreign priests. Buddhists desperate to keep Christianity from becoming Japan's leading religion tossed converts into boiling hot springs or suspended them upside down in a pit of excrement until they died, a process that could last for weeks with a tantalizing option offered: those who lifted a hand to renounce Christianity would be pulled out.

Christians finally rose in the Amakusa Rebellion of December 1637, but 100,000 troops overwhelmed the Christian army of 37,000 at the castle of Hara on April 12, 1638. A complete massacre followed. Over the next 250 years persecution continued, with Buddhist priests reporting every year any information they had about Christians in their areas, and officials offering large rewards for information leading to the capture of Christians. One Kyoto museum includes a public notice on wood offering five hundred silver coins for denunciation of a priest down to one hundred for a catechist; these notices were common from the 1600s through the mid-nineteenth century.

The threat of Christianity was so great that even angry Nichiren adherents and sardonic Zen Buddhists agreed to join hands in a national Buddhist parish system. From the seventeenth century to the late nineteenth century, Buddhist temples took charge of the official annual census; each January every Japanese adult in Nagasaki and some other areas had to show his rejection of Christianity by trampling on a crucifix or a *fumie,* a picture on metal of Christ or his mother Mary. A Nagasaki museum today displays twenty bronze fumies cast by an engraver from metal obtained from the altars of demolished churches.

Buddhist leaders such as Shosan Suzuki, author of anti-Christian attack pieces in the seventeenth century, knew that an increasingly corrupt Buddhist priesthood could not become the centerpiece of a Japanese culture able to turn back foreign ideas. Shosan proposed an alternative, telling merchants to "throw yourself headlong into worldly activity. . . . Your activity is an ascetic exercise that will cleanse you of all impurities. Challenge your mind and body by crossing mountain ranges. Purify your heart by fording rivers."

Shosan, now called "the founder of Japanese capitalism," provided a theology for merchants: "If you understand that this life is but a trip through an evanescent world, and if you cast aside all attachments and desires and work hard, Heaven will protect you, the gods will bestow their favor, and your profits will be exceptional." He stressed that "all occupations are Buddhist practice. Through work we are able to attain Buddhahood." Another priest praised the merchants' nonattachment: "They go out early in the morning and return late at night. They do not avoid the elements nor do they dislike hardship and misery. They cover their bodies with cotton clothing and fill their mouths with vegetable food. They do not dare to throw away a piece of thread or a scrap of paper."

Other Buddhist priests also praised the nonattachment of one merchant, Takata Zenemon, because "carrying lamp-wicks and bamboo hats, he went out into the mountain districts. . . . He diligently for over 50 years exerted himself practicing strenuous economy. But with honesty as a basis, he worked without minding labor that was hard to endure and was answered with heavenly considerations." One seventeenth-century book, *Shimin Nichiyo,* answered questions such as this one from an artisan: "I am busy every minute of the day in an effort to earn my livelihood. How can I become a Buddha?" The answer: "Do not neglect diligent activity morning and evening. Work hard at the family occupation. Do not gamble. Rather than take a lot, take a little."

At first such teaching was seen as useful for those without a priestly vocation; but as corruption within Buddhism increased, secular activities started to be seen as equally worthy to religious ones, and eventually as superior. Ishida Baigan in the early eighteenth century argued that merchants should have high social status, for they follow "the way of the townsman" that is more socially useful than the way of the priest or the samurai. Hosoi Heishu, late in the eighteenth century, lectured throughout Japan on the way that people in everyday tasks could show the modesty, diligence, and frugality that create good karma.

Within Mahayana Buddhist understanding, just as bodhisattvas showed their nonattachment to Nirvana by a willingness to sacrifice their own welfare, so businessmen could also be above it all: "The business of merchants and of artisans is the profiting of others. By profiting others they receive the right to profit themselves. . . . The spirit of profiting others is the bodhisattva spirit. Having a bodhisattva spirit and saving all beings, this is called bodhisattva deeds. . . . The secret of merchants and artisans' business lies in obtaining confidence through bodhisattva deeds."

For over two centuries, then, entrepreneurship has been the moral equivalent of war. War itself commanded Japan's attention from the 1930s through 1945, but since then company and government campaigns have taken the place of military battles. Japan's big government and big business leaders show their Buddhist backgrounds in many ways, such as by calling briefing sessions on new pieces of legislation *okyo-yomi,* sutra-chanting. Two out of five Japanese adult males are "salarymen" who work all day in a corporate or government office and are obligated to spend most evenings with business associates. Part of their *kugyo,* hard practice, is travel three hours per day because land close to city centers is prohibitively expensive. Wives, typically charged with keeping homes pristine and children disciplined and increasingly taking part-time jobs to gain income or satisfy occupational longings, have their own *kugyo.*

And for what? Veteran missionary Mark Dominey, who lives in a thirty-five-floor apartment building in the Tokyo area with a thousand other people, notes that salarymen don't arrive home until eleven on the average: "After work comes eating, drinking, and playing with bar hostesses. Often, children only see their fathers on Sundays." Some students at Kyoto International University told me that they hardly saw their fathers on Sundays either: the fathers were so tired that they slept much of the day.

Nonattachment has an impact in other ways. When husbands are transferred by their companies, families often stay behind, and husbands live alone in an uncomfortable existence called *tanshin-funin.* Some left-behind wives assume their husbands will take mistresses. It's hard to miss the "love motels" that have spread throughout Japan and are reportedly prosperous even as many restaurants and retail stores have gone under during the past decade of recession. Many young Japanese, seeing the loveless relationships of their parents, are finding the prospect of marriage and family unattractive. Japan's birthrate is down to its lowest level ever, with officials projecting that Japan's current population of 127 million will decline to 101 million by the year 2050.

How much of Japan's malaise stems from Buddhism and its nonattachment principle is debatable; after all, Shintoism and other ideological and theological currents are present in Japan, and the United States, founded on a different theology, has some similar problems. When Japan was on an economic winning streak from the 1960s (when it achieved its goal of doubling national income within the decade) to 1990, *ware ware Nihon-jin* (roughly translated as "we Japanese, we together") became a popular expression. But many Japanese have seen the Buddhist tradition, with its anti-individualistic emphasis on *wa* rather than a war on corruption, as a leading culprit.

The thought expressed by "the buck stops here" is not popular in Japan, where an emphasis on shared responsibility often means that the buck stops nowhere. Nonattachment can lead to courage, but it can also mean that no one cares deeply enough to risk a career for a principle. As the Japanese government has sustained insolvent banks and insurance companies, needed readjustments—such as writing off bad bank loans and emphasizing competition rather than government protectionism in farming and construction—have not come.

One recent Tokyo best seller, *The Straitjacket Society*, decried Japan's collectivist emphases and complained that "the bureaucracy controls the entire market through a system of regulations and permits." Author Masao Miyamoto noted that companies frequently hire retired bureaucrats in a practice known as *amakudari* (literally, "descended from heaven") to oppose deregulation that could create new competition. Regulators, assured of fat jobs if they see no evil, ignore deception. Miyamoto expressed pessimism about Japan's economic future, for change "would mean downsizing and restructuring, to which the bureaucrats would never agree."

Individual initiative is now unpopular not only in government but also in philanthropy. Japan's large government sector dominates social services even more than its U.S. counterpart does. It's been difficult in Japan to form charities apart from government, and givers receive no tax incentives. Lack of philanthropic initiative seems to have a religious base, as Buddhist priest Shojun Bando acknowledged: "The basis of Buddhist teaching is *karuna,* compassion, but to what extent that is lived by people, by alleged Buddhists, is questionable. *Karuna* must be realized in concrete ways. . . . In that respect Buddhism is far behind Christianity."

Rejection of the straitjacket has led some to the opposite extreme. Japanese talk of teen disenchantment and an increase of graffiti, theft, and chaotic classrooms. Twenty years ago students would wait to go to the bathroom or, in cases of desperate need, would raise a hand tentatively. Now they get up and go. Once any kind of incivility on trains or buses was taboo; now some people eat in those public conveyances and occasionally get into fights. So economics and culture work on each other in what can readily become a downward societal spiral. A 2002 cover story in *Newsweek's* Asia edition captured the mood: "Japan Takes It Easy: The Former Juggernaut Seems Destined to Become Asia's Switzerland—Rich, Comfortable and Irrelevant."

Japan has taken nonattachment in two secular directions—one which first produced military success and then disaster, and one which first produced economic success and then trouble. Now, unless Japan can generate faster economic growth and end its debt dependence, an immense crisis is likely. This includes the possibility of a debt default, with lenders refusing to lend because they don't believe the debt can be serviced. This could bankrupt financial institutions that already hold government debt. Just because Japan is richer than Argentina does not mean it is invulnerable to a comparable financial collapse, with cultural and religious effects hard to predict.

What happens to whole societies when centers do not hold? Look at a few headlines from one Japanese tabloid for one recent day:

- Woman Hurt After Hit by Man Taking Death Leap
- Plastic-bag Encased Body Dumped on Construction Site
- Wanted Bank Robber Nabbed on Kumamoto Highway
- Cop Sacked for Stealing Pricey Camera
- Woman Kills Newborn with Mouthful of Toilet Paper

- 75-year-old Man Tries to Throttle Centenarian Mother
- Health Food Company Defrauds 3,000 Investors.

Even keeping in mind press hype, that list is an indication of the variety of problems that are pushing more Japanese to think anew about when to be attached and to what.

Polls show most Japanese having little regular contact with any religion, but Buddhism still is basic in Japan and even the Japanese language. Some say that the Japanese word for "thank you," *arigato*, is a splicing of *aru* (your existence) and *katai* (very difficult). Buddhism teaches that we are condemned to a material existence and enslaved by attachments, so *arigato* means, "I am thankful for this which allows me to exist in such a difficult situation." (Others say that *arigato* is derived from the Portuguese *obrigado*, "thanks," but that would also be culturally significant: For centuries Japanese had no word for "thank you," since whatever a person did was seen to be his dharma duty.)

The difference between intellectual and popular understandings of what allows us to exist amid difficulty is immense. Zen theologians may refer to the sound of one hand clapping; but near the Kongobun-ji Temple on Mount Koya-san, Japanese visitors use their hands to pick up pine needles and stick them in their wallets, superstitiously hoping that wealth will come. Others at a nearby cemetery pick up big rocks, an action that will purportedly lead to wishes being granted by some cosmic force. Others meditate before a container that houses a lock of hair from each emperor over the centuries: Do that, some say, and the visitor will walk away with a bit of the emperors' godstuff.

Not far from the sanctified hair stand some statues of Buddhist heroes. Adults and children who use ladles to splash water on the faces of the statues explain in three different ways why they are doing that. Some simply say it's fun to do. Others say that if they give the hero a drink he will use his power to help a person buried nearby. Others say that the loved person who has died is now in some way suffering with a dry throat, and tossing some water on the statues gives the dead a drink. This is considered a particularly effective tactic if the mourner has written on a paper the deceased's name and made a donation to the Buddhist temple nearby.

It's hard to say how any of this makes sense in terms of either transmigration or the lack of a personal God in Buddhism. Nevertheless, at the cemetery temple mourners can pay the equivalent of about $42 to priests so they will recite a prayer for the dead person. If a mourner pays the equivalent of $420 and brings the Adam's apple bone (which almost always survives cremation) of the recently deceased, the priests will keep it for a year and pray over it. A person without much money can buy a prayer stick made of wood and burn it, supposedly to purify his heart; bad things will stay away from those with pure hearts. Corporate statues—including one for Nissan and another for a large coffee company—dot the cemetery.

Today on Mount Hiei overlooking Kyoto, where Buddhist armies once ruled, monks still do *kugyo* for nine days in two linked temples: Jogyo-Do (constant walking) and

Hokke-Do (sitting meditation). When meditating they fast, drink only a little water, and try hard not to fall asleep; as one monk explained the goal, "If we can remove the desire for food or sleep, we can get closer to the goal of leaving behind all desire." Another Mt. Hiei temple, Shyaka-do, is the base for elite monks who are supposed to walk for at least eighteen miles a day for one hundred days up and down the mountain's steep slopes. Others, wearing straw sandals, try to do a thousand days of walking fifty miles a day. (The monks I asked were vague on how often this was done over the centuries or how often it's done now.)

Overall on Mount Koya-san, a thousand monks in 120 temples show that they are not attached to normal pleasures. When we spoke, the head monk noted sadly that the mountain in feudal times boasted of five thousand priests in one thousand temples. Even when he was young, the head monk said, he and other novices walked six miles back and forth to a work site, wearing geta (wood sandals). Today priests keep up appearances, starting the day at six with a sutra chanting in a dark temple filled with hypnotic intensity and the smell of incense and then walking the six miles to the work site, but they do so in running shoes, and they receive a ride back.

Buddhism Time Line over the Past Two Thousand Years

67 AD Two monks bring Buddhism to China.

100 Mahayana Buddhism emerges as a separate school of Buddhism.

148 First translations of Indian Buddhist texts into Chinese.

320 Vajrayana Buddhism, with its emphasis on mantra reciting, emerges.

400 Over five thousand monks are studying at the University of Nalanda in Northern India. They plant Buddhism in many countries, including Myanmar and Indonesia.

520 In China, Bodhidharma founds Chan (Zen) Buddhism.

550 Buddhism becomes Korea's state religion and also enters Japan and Vietnam around this time.

625 Shotoku makes Buddhism a Japanese state religion.

632 Tibet declares Buddhism to be the state religion.

719 Buddhism, declining in India, is introduced to Thailand.

800 By this time Buddhist texts have been translated into Greek, Syriac, Arabic, and many other languages.

803 Tendai sect founded in Japan.

806 Kobo Daishi (Kukai) introduces Shingon Buddhism to Japan.

845 Chinese Emperor Wu-tsung orders that all Buddhist establishments be destroyed.

1075 Burma's King Anoratha adheres to Theravada Buddhism and pressure others to join him.

1181 Jayavarman VII, who calls himself a bodhisattva, becomes king of the Khmers (Cambodians).

1250 Jodo Shin (Pure Land Truth) sect emerges in Japan, with an emphasis on relying on Buddha's grace rather than personal effort.

1253 Nichiren founds a Japanese Buddhist sect, named after him, that attacks all other forms of Buddhism.

1400 Decline of adherents in India leaves Buddhism a rarity in its place of birth.

1450 Gyalwa Gendun Drubpa serves as the first Dalai Lama of Tibet.

1600 Muslims eradicate Buddhism in Indonesia.

1637 Buddhists ally with shogun in massacre of Japanese Christians.

1650 Buddhists in Sri Lanka undergo persecution and are nearly eradicated.

1750 Hakuin Zenji reforms Zen Buddhism in Japan.

1840 Ming Mang, reigning in Vietnam, restricts dissemination of Buddhist materials and orders all monks to carry identification papers.

1881 Forming of Pali Text Society in England leads to translation and publication in English of Buddhist scriptures.

1893 Parliament of World Religions in Chicago publicizes Buddhism (and Hinduism).

1950 Chinese Communists conquer their land and try to wipe out Buddhism.

1975 Cambodian Communists led by Pol Pot try to destroy Buddhism by killing nearly every monk and burning Buddhist libraries.

Chapter Seven

Islam and Attachment

Jews and Muslims are often at each other's throats these days, but they have a similar appeal for those seeking a rule-based structure to life. Islam, like Judaism, also has strong appeals of other kinds as well, starting with its iron-clad monotheism. Muslims believe in one god, all-powerful and ever present, uncreated, without beginning or end, completely sufficient to himself, and ordaining everything that occurs. The power of Islam moved Arabs and many other people from polytheism, often accompanied by grotesque practices, to monotheism.

Islam is different from Judaism in that Judaism through most of its history has emphasized ethnic connections with one particular people, but Islam has gained probably one billion adherents—only 15 percent of them Arabs—by welcoming adherents of every skin color and ethnicity. Muslims have had their own problems with racial reconciliation, given the history of Arab development of the slave trade; but the Quran, like the Bible, is colorblind. The several million Muslims now living in the United States can trace their ancestry back to many countries of Asia, Africa, and Europe. That appeal has been strong, particularly when some churches made their peace with racism.

Muslims, like strict constructionist Jews, cite chapter and verse to support statements they make; the 114 chapters (*suras*) of the Quran (which in Arabic means "the reading") take the place of the five books of Moses. Muslims fight *shirk*, which is an attempt to attribute Allah's qualities to anyone or anything else. It is *shirk*, a sin, to think or say that anyone else can bring rain, satisfy desire, or cause babies to be born. It is *shirk* to believe that anyone else has godlike knowledge or to seek information from astrologers, palm readers, or the like.

Islam's most distinctive appeal is that, instead of teaching Buddhistlike nonattachment or Jewish-style intellectualism, it highly values attachment to the material pleasures of this life. Islam promises that if a person believes in Allah, has accumulated good deeds that exceed his bad deeds, and sincerely repents of his sins, he will go to heaven (S 3:135; 7:8–9; 21:47; 49:14; and 66:8–9); otherwise his destiny is hell. Saved souls will be in a blissful garden that has fruit, carpets and cushions, rivers, and sensual pleasure (S 3:198; 4:57; 55:56; 56:35–38; 69:21–24; 79:41; 88:8–16). Women will offer righteous men great sensual gratification: "For the Righteous there will be a fulfillment of desires, gardens enclosed, and grapevines, and voluptuous women" (S 78:31–33).

Current Muslim commentators hasten to add that women will also have whatever they desire. One notes that the Quran says everyone in the next life will be fully rewarded for his good deeds in this life. That means each person, male or female, shall get all he desires, including having a perfect sexual partner as a reward for his deeds. As one Muslim commentator put it, if a person controls himself in this life, Allah "in His infinite mercy shall grant him all that he desired to get but from which he refrained himself."

Muslims, emphasizing the material, developed a civilization that made great advances in science and medicine. They emphasized health through rules of cleanliness and diet. In medieval times they emphasized medical research because Muhammad had taught that "God has not created an illness without creating a cure for it . . . some already known and some are not." Some Muslim commentators also have tried to merge material and spiritual analyses by connecting to the Big Bang one Quranic statement: "Have not the disbelievers seen that the Heavens and the Earth were one piece and we parted them? And we made every living thing from water" (S 21:30).

The Muslim pleasure with material benefits also leads to an emphasis on holidays, not hair shirts. The one major time of deprivation, the month of Ramadan during which Muslims are not to eat from dawn to dusk, ends with Eid-ul-Fitr, a three-day festival of fast-breaking marked by celebrations with relatives and friends and frequently the giving of gifts and money to children. Another holiday, Eid-ul-Adha, is a four-day commemoration of what Muslims say was Abraham's willingness to submit to Allah even to the extent of killing his son Ishmael (not Isaac, according to the Quran).

Another appeal of Islam is its easy entry process: a person desiring to be a Muslim should simply declare, "There is no God but Allah, and Muhammad is his Prophet." Mosques and Islamic foundations will then offer instruction in the Five Pillars of Islam. The first pillar is to offer that declaration about Allah and Muhammad regularly. The second: pray five times daily while facing Mecca. The third: no drinking, eating, or sexual relations during the daylight hours of the month of Ramadan, believed to be the month Muhammad received the first revelation of the Quran. Fourth pillar: Muslims are to give 2.5 percent of their saved earnings to charity each year or more if they feel moved. The fifth pillar: make a pilgrimage to Mecca at least once, if economically and physically able, and do it during the first half of the last month of the lunar year.

Islam also has the advantage of displaying a clear founder, and adherents do not argue about the dates of his life. Muslims acclaim Muhammad Ibn Abdullah (c. 570–632 AD) as the last and greatest prophet. They honor him as a direct descendent of Prince Kedar, the second son of Abraham's son Ishmael. Orphaned at the age of six, raised by his uncle, and put to work as a shepherd and then a camel driver, Muhammad traveled between Arabia and Syria. He learned about Judaism, Christianity, and pagan religions, and meditated on them in the melting pot of his mind.

Muslims say Muhammad received the revelation of the Quran from the angel Jibreel (Gabriel) in 610 AD and became a strong defender of the autonomy and uniqueness of Allah. He took on the task of moving his countrymen from polytheism and decadence to monotheism and morality, but his countrymen initially opposed him. In 622 AD, facing persecution in Mecca, Muhammad escaped 275 miles north to Yathrib, an oasis village later renamed Medina, the city of the prophet. (Muslims today follow a lunar calendar that starts with this trip, called the Hijra.) Jews in Medina antagonized him by rejecting his message, but Muhammad, knocking off opponents as necessary, unified the nomadic Arab tribes before his death in 632 AD.

Since Muhammad appointed no successor, Muslims soon disagreed about whether future caliphs could come from among Muhammad's tribesmen (the position of the Sunni, which became the largest sect) or whether they had to be the descendants of Ali, Muhammad's son-in-law (the view of the Shiites, who became the second-large division). Three of the first four caliphs to succeed Muhammad suffered assassination. Nevertheless, Islam's expansion over the next century was fast. By 732 Islam was known in China and dominant in Spain. Had Charles "the Hammer" Martel not led Europeans that year to a victory over Islam in the battle of Poitiers/Tours, Islam might have conquered all of Europe.

The early Islamic empires grew through persuasion plus force; the exact percentages are in dispute. The basic Quranic principle is that people should freely declare their allegiance to Allah, and that often happened when other religions were only nominally held and Islam seemed to be on an unstoppable winning streak. When those conquered were not so obliging, in some cases they had the choice of praising Allah or dying by way of a sword to the gut.

Military efforts gained a great impetus from the Quran, which teaches that "truly Allah loves those who fight in His Cause in battle array, as if they were a solid cemented structure" (S 61:4). The Quran particularly condemns what today we would call draft dodgers: "O ye who believe! what is the matter with you, that, when ye are asked to go forth in the cause of Allah, ye cling heavily to the earth? Do ye prefer the life of this world to the Hereafter? But little is the comfort of this life, as compared with the Hereafter. Unless ye go forth, He will punish you with a grievous penalty, and put others in your place" (S 9:38–39; 4:74–76; 61:10–12).

Along with its attitude toward warfare, Islam was helped in its early years by its smiling attitude toward accumulation of wealth. At a time when some Christians were saying that poverty is godly, within Islam it was (and is) fine to be attached to a business and to enjoy wealth, as long as funds are gained lawfully and one-fortieth of savings are given to charity each year. Muslims forbid cheating and stealing and emphasize rights of ownership; Islam and socialism do not logically mix, although the Baath parties in Iraq and Syria tried to meld the two.

Today Islam appeals not only to progressives resentful of Christianity or other religions but also to many who rebel against modernism and the materialistic theories that dominate America. For example, Orthodox Islam is strongly creationist, stating that Allah created the universe in six days and sustains it through his permission and will (Suras 2:29; 3:191; 6:1; 25:61–62; 36:81; 46:33). The six days may have been equal to huge numbers of years. Man is superior to nature but is to cultivate and protect land and animals. Mohammad taught that cultivating land brings earthly and heavenly rewards, that destroying trees as a means of warfare is not allowed, and that "no bird or animal is to be killed except for food."

Muslims use both the Quran and the evidence of intelligent design within nature to critique evolutionists. Once, when a Bedouin was asked what made him believe in Allah, he pointed to marks in the sand, which made clear to him that a camel had gone by, even though he had not seen the camel. He then pointed to the mountains and said that it was equally clear that Allah had made them, although he did not witness that either. So Muslims say that the beauty and order of the universe, as well as the integration and complexity of a single cell, show intelligent design. They say that such complexity could not be the product merely of time plus chance.

For those rebelling against modernism, Islam's social conservatism is also appealing. The Quran specifically attacks the killing of children, using an Arabic word, *awlad*, that translates as "born and unborn children." Muslims say that if the prohibition only concerned born children, the word *mawlood*, "born children," used elsewhere in the Quran, would have been used. Instead, Sura 17:31 is clear: "And do not kill your children (*awlad*) for fear of poverty; we give them sustenance, and yourselves; surely to kill them is a great wrong."

Some modernized Muslims say abortion should be allowed during the first three months of pregnancy (S 23:11) when the health of the mother is in jeopardy and when economic constraints are overwhelming. Most stick with the Quran's emphasis on the continual development of the unborn child as part of Allah's will. "We created you from dust, then from a small seed, then from a clot, then from a lump of flesh," Sura 22:5 reads. "Then We bring you forth as babies."

The Quran refers five times to gay and lesbian behavior. The two main references are: "Ye practice your lusts on men in preference to women: ye are indeed a people transgressing beyond bounds" (Q 7:81) and "Do ye come unto the males, and leave the wives your Lord created for you? Nay, but ye are forward folk" (Q 26:165). The first verse is a reference to Sodom; the Quran links its destruction to its homosexual practice.

Supporting the Quran are the Hadith, the stories about Muhammad's life that Muslim leaders two centuries later considered reputable. For example, the Hadith have Muhammad saying, concerning male homosexuality, "When a man mounts another man, the throne of God shakes"; when told about two male partners, Muhammad orders his followers to "kill the one that is doing it and also kill the one that it is being done to." With some loose constructionist churches embracing homosexuality, Islam's stand has had strong appeal for those wanting a strong stand against sin.

That has been particularly true in the United States, where leaders such as Dr. Muzammil Siddiqi of the Islamic Society of North America have pulled no punches: "Homosexuality is a moral disorder. It is a moral disease, a sin and corruption. . . . No person is born homosexual, just like no one is born a thief, a liar or murderer. People acquire these evil habits due to a lack of proper guidance and education. . . . Homosexuality is dangerous for the health of the individuals and for the society. It is a main cause of one of the most harmful and fatal diseases. It is disgraceful for both men and women. It degrades a person. Islam teaches that men should be men and women should be women. Homosexuality deprives a man of his manhood and a woman of her womanhood. It is the most unnatural way of life."

But as we dive deeper into Islam, it becomes apparent that the Muslim definition of what is natural differs greatly from the Christian one. Christians argue that, ever since Adam and Eve's sin in the garden of Eden, it has been natural for man to sin, and the only way to reverse that natural process is through the intervention of the supernatural—the work of God's grace because of Christ's sacrifice. The Quran, though, states that in the garden of Eden Adam and Eve both sinned, then repented and were forgiven, with no consequences from their rebellion: "Adam learnt from his Lord certain words and his Lord forgave him." Allah then makes Adam his deputy (caliph) and the first of the prophets.

The backstory provides more detail. Islam has its own set of angels and jinn, created out of light and fire, respectively (S 15:27; 51:56; 55:15). Both sets of creatures live in an unseen world, but angels are sinless and carry out Allah's commands, while jinn can be good or bad. Muslims tell of how jealousy led Iblis (the devil) to become an evil jinn: When Allah created Adam, he commanded the angels, and Satan from the jinn, to prostrate before Adam as a sign of respect, although not a sign of worship. All except Satan did so. When Allah asked Satan why he disobeyed, Satan replied, "I am better than Adam, you created him from Clay and created me from Fire" (S 2:34). Allah cursed Satan, and Satan pledged to destroy Adam and his descendants.

Crucially, then, Islam does not acknowledge original sin. Muslims say they revere the whole Bible, but when it and the Quran are in conflict, they go with the Quran. That means Muslims have a tendency to revere strong leaders who put forth an image of perfection; Christians, realizing that all have sinned and fall short of God's glory, tend to be skeptical.

Christians read in the Bible honest reporting about twisted, sinful individuals whom God chose not because of their own righteousness but because of his love. Muslims, though, see a record of great heroes that Jews and Christians somehow twisted during centuries of transmission. What to Christians makes the Bible ring true—its record of how Noah got drunk, Lot committed incest, etc.—parts of it ring false to Muslims. Muslims believe that biblical leaders must have been picked by Allah to carry his messages because of their strong character. Christians emphasize God's grace in changing people like Jacob and Joseph who were liars and braggarts.

The difference between the Quran and the Bible is profound. The God of the Bible knows our sinful frames and is grieved by our disobedience. He is portrayed as a husband who feels pain because of an unfaithful wife or a father brokenhearted by his children's rebellion. Allah, on the other hand, is described as all merciful, and indeed he sends prophets who warn people; but if those people disobey, so be it. The Noah stories of the Quran and the Bible provide a good basis for comparison. In Sura 71 of the Quran, Noah warns his people, they disobey, they drown in the flood. Game, set, match. Same thing happens in the Bible, but there God's "heart was filled with pain" (Gen. 6:6).

The Bible, in short, emphasizes that God adopts us into his family. The Quran emphasizes that a just master allows us to be his servants but not his children. Biblical passages about God's majesty have their parallels in the Quran, but look at the biblical passages that emphasize God's tenderness, showing him as a father who teaches his child to walk or as a shepherd carrying his lamb in his arms (Deut. 1:31; Hosea 11:1–4; Isa. 40:11). Those do not have their parallels in the Quran.

This leads to the most important contrast. The Old Testament—chapter 53 of Isaiah—describes the most important character in history in this way: "He was despised and rejected by men, a man of sorrows and familiar with suffering. . . . he was pierced for our transgressions, he was crushed for our iniquities; the punishment that brought us peace was upon him, and by his wounds we are healed" (vv. 3, 5). The New Testament, in Hebrews 4, makes clear the significance of this: "We do not have a high priest who is unable to sympathize with our weaknesses, but we have one who has been tempted in every way, just as we are—yet was without sin. Let us then approach the throne of grace with confidence, so that we may receive mercy and find grace to help us in our time of need" (vv. 16–17).

Muslims respect the rejected and wounded Jesus Christ as one of perhaps 124,000 messengers or prophets Allah has sent and one of the twenty-five listed in the Quran. Jesus is right there in the list with Adam, Enoch, Noah, Abraham, Ishmael, Isaac, Lot, Jacob, Joseph, Job, Moses, Aaron, Ezekiel, David, Solomon, Elijah, Elisha, Jonah, Zechariah, John, three others not cited in the Bible, and Muhammad. But Muslims do not believe Jesus died when crucified. They do not believe he was resurrected. They do not see him as God.

Within Islam that unbiblical depiction makes logical sense: Since there is no original sin, there is no need for a redeemer. Man is basically good but mistake prone; Muslims who sincerely repent and submit to Allah return to a state of sinlessness, with no help from Christ needed. Man, using his intelligence and guided by the Quran, can distinguish good from evil. Sincerity and good works bring salvation: As Sura 7:8–9 states, "For him whose measure (of good deeds) is heavy, those are they who shall be successful."

But if original sin does not exist, why does the Bible tell the stories of so many sinners? Muslims treat the Bible respectfully as the word of prophets but see it as corrupted through the centuries and only right when it agrees with the Quran. Muslims also believe that all people are sinless unless they specifically rebel against Allah. Since sin is so serious, Christians do not believe that any works are sufficient to merit salvation; Muslims believe that faith in Allah plus actions make salvation effective.

Christianity pushes for more than people can naturally produce, so God's grace is necessary. Islam does not require more than is naturally achievable. A Christian who dies and stands before God cannot point to any of his good deeds and hope to get into heaven because of them; he must rely on grace. A Muslim can say he deserves entry into heaven because he has submitted to Allah's law and thus deserves Allah's mercy. Angels will have recorded his good deeds as well as his bad.

Muslims say man is good but will go wrong if given freedom. Christians want man to be given enough freedom to come close to hanging himself, so that realizing his sin he turns to God. Muslims must strictly obey the laws of the Quran and all teachings of Mohammed. By observing the Five Pillars and other regulations, they exhibit faith in Allah, sincere repentance, and obedience to Islamic law (S 3:135; 7:8–9; 21:47; 49:14; 66:8–9).

Muslims are also to abstain from a variety of things seen as harmful, including eating pork and gambling. Islam bans consumption of drugs, because they are seen as distorting thought, but also alcohol, with no distinction between drinking a glass of wine and getting drunk. The emphasis within Islamic thinking has often been on behavioral conformity (orthopraxy) rather than doctrinal conformity (orthodoxy). Muslims are to ask themselves every day WWMD: what would Muhammad do? Believers try to sleep, eat, drink, and even dress as he did. They try to repeat the special prayers he uttered upon going to sleep and waking up, or even upon entering and leaving the bathroom.

The pilgrimage to Mecca is particularly important, as Muhammad stated that someone who performs it properly "will return as a newly born baby," free of all sins. Doing it properly means entering the holy mosque at Mecca with the right foot first and reciting a prayer, then moving in a counterclockwise procession around a stone building that Muslims believe Abraham and his son Ishmael originally built. The pilgrim also performs the *sa'I,* which means hurrying seven times between two small hills that are near Mecca in order to commemorate the desperate search for water by Ishmael's mother Hagar. Other ritual events include throwing seven pebbles at a pillar to commemorate what the Quran says was Satan's tempting of Abraham to disobey Allah's command and not kill his son.

Since Muslims think we can be sinless if we have strong character and follow all the rules, the rules (mostly taken from the Hadith) get more and more specific. Some of these are terrific, emphasizing humility: Don't boast about how you've contributed to build a mosque. Don't set up elaborate grave markers. Don't wear clothes just designed to attract attention. Some are incredibly precise: Do not eradicate insects by burning them because fire is to be used only on rats, scorpions, crows, kites, and mad dogs. Do not read the Quran in a house where there is a dog unless the dog is used for hunting, farming, or herding livestock.

The nature of Islamic prayer periods during the day is also rule driven. Each time of prayer is made up of units containing set sequences of standing, bowing, kneeling, and prostrating while reciting verses from the Quran or other prayer formulas. The sequences are repeated twice at dawn prayer, three times at sunset prayer, and four times at noon, afternoon, and evening prayers. No deviation is allowed. Muslims do not gain from their religion a sense of liberty.

Overall Islamic law and tradition provide an enormous list of what to do and what not to do. Some prohibitions are designed to protect the sanctity of prayer: for example, Muslims are not to pray when they urgently need a bathroom break because that pressure would distract a person from concentrating properly on his prayer. Others emphasize humility: Islam forbids boasting about good deeds or the contributions made to building a mosque. (If you boast, Allah does not give you credit for your effort.) Mosques are not to be decorated with red or yellow paint. Muslims are forbidden to build over graves, make them high, put lights over them, or write on them. Men are not to wear gold, and no one is to wear clothes that attract attention.

Some rules are for reasons of health and safety. Muslims are not to urinate into stagnant water or defecate on the side of the road or in places where people seek shade or where they draw water. A Muslim is not to put a hand into any vessel before washing it when he has just woken up. Men are not to hold penises in their right hand when urinating because that's the hand used in greeting others. A Muslim is forbidden to hold small stones between two fingers and throw them because this could cause injury to eyes or teeth. A Muslim is not to walk through the marketplace carrying a sharp weapon unless it is properly covered.

Islam, like Judaism, precisely details what is allowed and what is not in daily life. Today Web sites are filled with detailed questions and answers about dos and don'ts. For example, one questioner asked a cleric, "Is it permissible to kill insects that may be found in the house, such as ants, cockroaches and the like, by burning them? If it is not permissible, what should we do?" The answer was, "If these insects are harmful, they may be killed with insecticides, but not with fire." That's because fire, according to Muhammad, was to be used on rats, scorpions, crows, kites [like hawks], and mad dogs.

The detail soon becomes overwhelming. Categories of law codes on www.al-islam.org/laws include specifics on "Pure and Mixed Water, Kurr Water, Under-Kurr Water, Running Water, Rain Water, [and] Well Water." The "Urine and Feces" section includes specifics on "Semen, Dead Body, Blood, Dogs and Pigs," and so on. Headings under "Things which make a fast void" include "Sexual Intercourse, Istimna [Masturbation], Ascribing Lies to Allah and His Prophet, Letting Dust Reach One's Throat, Immersing One's Head in Water, Enema, [and] Vomiting."

Also, under the heading "Method of Slaughtering Animals," categories include "Conditions of Slaughtering Animals, Method of Slaughtering a Camel, Mustahab Acts while Slaughtering Animals, Makrooh Acts while Slaughtering Animals, Hunting with Weapons, Hunting with a Retriever (Hunting Dog), Hunting of Fish and Locust, Rules of Things Allowed to Eat and Drink, Eating Manners, Acts Which Are Unworthy to Do While Taking a Meal,

Manners of Drinking Water." Under "Conditions of a Seller and a Buyer" come "Conditions Regarding Commodity and what is Obtained in Exchange, Formula of Purchase and Sale, Purchase and Sale of Fruits, Cash and Credit, Conditions for Contract by Advance Payment, Laws Regarding Advance Payment Contract, Sale of Gold and Silver against Gold and Silver, When One Has a Right to Cancel a Transaction," and so forth.

That list only suggests the great multitude of rules. All in all, about 10 percent of the Quran's six thousand verses contain injunctions that Islamic scholars have converted into religious or legal requirements. The Quran includes food requirements (generally similar to those involving Jews who keep kosher, except that alcohol is forbidden), rules concerning marriage and divorce, penalties for crimes, and commercial regulations including a ban on *riba* (usury). Islam's many dietary restrictions, prohibitions of certain kinds of sexual activities, and other rules seem arbitrary to non-Muslims; but as one Web site states at the end of its long list, "There are more commands and prohibitions which came for the benefit and happiness of individuals and mankind as a whole."

Detailed rules also emphasize the importance of privacy. Muslims must not eavesdrop on people without their permission. A man is forbidden to look at the *awrah* (private parts) of another man, and a woman is forbidden to look at the *awrah* of another woman. It is forbidden to sit between two people without their permission or to greet only those whom one knows because both those known and those unknown should be greeted.

Those who don't keep the rules will quickly get detached from material pleasures and will be, after death, dropped into hell, a place of unlimited capacity (S 50:30), eternal torment (S 2:39; 14:17; 25:65; 39:26), fire (S 9:63; 11:16; 25:11–12; 104:6–7), and boiling water (S 38:55–58; 55:43–44). Unbelieving humans (S 3:13; 19:49) and jinn (S 11:119) both go there. Those who remain true to Christianity and Judaism by not believing in Allah will get what they deserve: "The unbelievers among the People of the Book and the pagans shall burn for ever in the fire of Hell. They are the vilest of all creatures" (S 98:1–8). Some Muslims say that other Muslims also go to hell.

Many Muslims today are Sunni Muslims who largely follow the teachings of one of four early Islamic legal schools (Hanifa, Shafi, Hanibal, and Malik). Many are comfortable living within largely secular societies as long as they can abide generally by the Quran and the Hadith, with interpretations and applications provided by a consensus of Muslims. Abu Hanifa, founder of the Hanifa school of thought over a millennium ago, said that "those who face in the direction of Mecca at prayer are true believers and no act of theirs can remove them from the faith."

Most Sunnis say that as long as a government does not prevent Muslims from carrying out their ritual duties, it should not be described as anti-Islamic, and no attempt should be made to overthrow it. But Sunnis who are members of the Wahhab sect, such as Osama bin Ladin, believe that any government that does not enforce the strict Quranic code is practicing treason to Islam and must be overthrown.

Other Muslims who hope for *shari'a,* the complete rule of islamic law (concerning both rituals and customary practices) are Shi'ites, followers of the Jafri school. They not only think that descendants of Muhammad's nephew Ali (who married Muhammad's daughter, Fatimah) should rule because they are part of the Prophet's bloodline, but they also believe that Allah gave Muslims a succession of Imams—perfect teachers—up to the twelfth, known as the Mahdi (guided one). They say he never died but went into hiding and is waiting for the right time to reappear and lead mankind to a time of peace and prosperity.

A small percentage of Muslims are Sufis, mystics who try to gain personal union with Allah and wisdom directly from him via rituals, dancing, and meditation. Sufiism (named after shirts of wool, *souf,* worn by some early adherents) arose a millennium ago in reaction to the Qurans's legalism and in an attempt to bring to Islam ideas from Neoplatonism and Buddhism Both Sunnis and Shi'ites can be Sufis, but some Sunnis do not consider Sufiism to be legitimate Muslim practice.

In the United States some minor groups have hit the headlines. The Black Muslim Movement became known for its depiction of Christianity as the religion of white oppressors. Elijah Muhammad (born Elijah Poole) taught blacks were racially superior to whites and that a racial war is inevitable. Recently many in the movement have returned to traditionally nonracist Islamic beliefs, but some such as Louis Farrakhan have followed his beliefs. Farrakhan's words, though, have hurt less than instruments of personal and mass destruction such as gasoline-filled airliners com-mandeered by Wahhabi Muslims of Saudi Arabia.

Whether Muslims are Sunni, Shiite, or something else, they are generally so desirous of promoting Allah's lordship that they become angry about passages that show God taking a human form. They are not pleased with biblical passages indicating that God walked with man in the garden of Eden, wrestled with Jacob, or came to earth as Jesus in human flesh. Muslims say that the pre-Muhammad prophet-messengers of Allah—including Jesus, but also Noah, Abraham, Moses, David, and many more—were sent only to particular nations, not for all people as Muhammad was. Muslims say apostles wrote down the message Jesus gave, known as Injeel, but those writings were by some means altered; only passages that agree with the Quran are seen as true.

Antibiblical scholars for two centuries have depicted the Bible as a cut-and-paste job by not particularly skilled edi-tors. That type of criticism has not gone far with the Quran because writers who critique the Quran lower their life expectancy, as the next chapter will show. The authorized view is still that we should have faith in the Quran because Allah literally spoke it to the angel Jibreel, who in turn gave it directly to Muhammad over a twenty-three-year period from the time Muhammad was forty years old. The words of the Quran, Muslims say, were memorized bit by bit by Muhammad as the angel spoke to him; Muhammad in turn dictated the message to a scribe. Further, Muhammad is said to have had his associates commit various chapters to memory, with an authentic Quran receiving compilation soon after Muhammad's death.

Muslim scholars such as Ibn Warraq (hiding out in France), and western scholars such as John Wansbrough and Patricia Crone, have now begun questioning that. Scholars are discussing the possible alteration of the Quran itself between the time of its hypothetical formulation in around AD 700 and the time between 850 and 900 that it took definitive form. So much time passed between Muhammad and the writing down of what he is said to have received that a full-fledged, highly publicized debate on the subject could unnerve many ordinary Muslims.

Islam Glossary

Note: Quran is the Muslim-preferred spelling for what is often written as *Koran. Muslim* is the preferred spelling for a follower of Islam. *Moslim* is not recommended because it is often pronounced "mawzlem," which sounds like an Arabic word for "oppressor." Some Western writers in the past have referred to Islam as "Mohammedism." This is deeply offensive to many Muslims, as the term might suggest that Mohammed the prophet was in some way divine. Mohammed and Muhammad are alternate spellings for his name.

Ali Muhammad's son-in-law and close advisor. He became Caliph in AD 656 with the support of followers known as the Shia ("party"). When he was murdered in 660 his supporters split from other Muslims and became known as Shiites. They call Ali the first Imam.

Ayatollah A Shiite so well versed in the Quran, the Hadith, and Sharia law that he is considered by his followers as the most learned person of his time period.

Caliph (Kalifa) Temporal (but not spiritual) leader of a Muslim nation or empire.

Dhimmis (People of the Book) Jews and Christians: They are still second-class citizens to Muslims, but they can worship as they wish and own property, unlike other non-Muslims. They cannot build new synagogues or churches, and they can be required to pay extra taxes and submit to a wide variety of humiliations.

Dome of the Rock Building in Jerusalem where the holy of holies of the temple is said to have stood.

Faqir A Sufi who is poor (or poor in spirit, humbling himself before Allah).

Five Pillars Five requirements for all Muslims: Shahadah (declaration), salat (prayer), sawm (fasting), zakat (alms-giving), and hajj (pilgrimage).

Hadith Stories about and sayings of Muhammad that were put together two centuries after his death.

Hajj The requirement that each Muslim go on a pilgrimage to Mecca; the fifth pillar of Islam.

Hijra The escape of Muhammad and his followers from Mecca to Medina in 622.

Ibrahim Arabic for Abraham, considered by Muslims to be the first person to submit himself to Allah; he is thus the first Muslim.

Imam Mosque worship leader in Sunni Islam, major spiritual leader in Shiite Islam.

Ismail Arabic name for Ishmael, son of Abraham and ancestor of the Arabs.

Jibreel The angel Gabriel, Allah's messenger to Muhammad.

Jinn Invisible beings created from fire and able to act in both good and evil ways.

Kaba A rectangular structure (20 feet by 30 feet by 50 feet high) in Mecca; all Muslims pray toward it.

Masjid Arabic word for mosque, a building for worship and community gatherings, particularly on Friday.

Mecca Town where Muhammad was born, now Islam's most holy site and the destination for at least once-in-a-lifetime pilgrimages.

Medina Town that welcomed Muhammad when he had to flee from Mecca in 622; he was buried in Medina, now considered Islam's second most holy city.

Minaret Tower attached to a mosque from which a muezzin issues the call to prayer.

Muezzin Man who stands on a minaret and calls Muslims to prayer five times a day.

Mullah Within Sunni Islam, a scholar learned in Sharia law.

Prophets Twenty-five major ones include Adam, Abraham, David, and Jesus, but their messages were all in some way corrupted. Muhammad is the last and greatest, the Seal of the Prophets who delivered the final and uncorrupted message of Allah.

Ramadan The ninth month of the Islamic year is considered the month when Muhammad received the first revelation of the Quran. Muslims fast during the daytime throughout the month.

Sawm Arabic word for fasting; fasting during the daylight hours of the month of Ramadan is one of the Five Pillars of Islam.

Shahada Central Muslim statement of faith: "There is no god but Allah [in Arabic, "La illahah illah 'lla"] and Muhammed is his Prophet" ["Wah Muhammadan rasulu 'llah"]. Saying the Shahada in Arabic with the desire to become a Muslim immediately makes a person one.

Shaikh Town official or head religious leader.

Sharia Islamic law; sometimes more broadly, Islamic morality and culture.

Shiite Muslims About 15 percent of Muslims worldwide, but dominant in Iran and Iraq. Shiites have specific historical beliefs but also the political sense that leaders should combine temporal and spiritual power.

Sufi Muslims Those who emphasize mystical ways to break down barriers between Allah and themselves so they can be more than servants to him.

Sunna Best behavior for a Muslim, based on the example set by Muhammad.

Sunni Islam Four-fifths of Muslims worldwide; they are likely not to fall into Shiite extremism, but exceptions include Wahhab Sunnis such as Usama bin Ladin.

Sura Arabic term for a chapter of the Quran.

Twelvers Largest branch of Shiite Islam, they believe that the twelfth Imam (the Mahdi) has been hidden by Allah and will return on Judgment Day as a Messiah figure.

Umma All those who have submitted themselves to Allah and form the worldwide community of Muslims.

Wahhab A Sunni sect that embraces terrorism against non-Muslims.

Wali An Islamic term for saint.

Zakat Arabic word for almsgiving and one of the five pillars of Islam. Muslims are to give 2.5 percent of their net wealth annually to help the poor.

Chapter Eight

Nonattachment to Grace

As Islam spread in the United States during the past several decades, some Americans began to view Muslims as next-door neighbors. The events of September 11, 2001, made almost all Americans feel that way. Suddenly it became essential to know whether our neighbors were berserk or the terrorists were a minority stain within a larger strain of peacefulness.

It soon became clear that the terrorists largely came out of the Sunni movement that was founded by Ibn Abdul Wahhab (1703–1792). Wahhabis from the start were willing to kill civilians who opposed them. They did just that in the city of Qarbala in 1801, leaving two thousand ordinary folks dead. In the nineteenth and early twentieth centuries, Wahhabis opposed the "decadence" of the Ottoman Turk empire. In recent years they have worked to overthrow "the American empire" and have trained a generation of students for that pursuit through a network of *madrassas* (religious boarding schools) funded by Saudi oil money.

The instructions some of the September 11 terrorists carried with them clearly showed Wahhabi emphases and interpretations: "Read al-Tawba and Anfal [traditional war chapters from the Quran] and reflect on their meanings and remember all of the things that Allah has promised for the martyrs. . . . Know that the gardens of paradise are waiting for you in all their beauty, and the women of paradise are waiting, calling out, 'Come hither, friend of God.' They have dressed in their most beautiful clothing."

The nonattachment to life that at least the lead terrorists showed, then, was not nonattachment to material pleasures, which they believed would be more abundant in paradise. Their nonattachment was to any hope of grace. Adherents to a religion of grace do not worry about being zapped at any moment for freelancing. Muslims, though, try to sleep, eat, drink, and even dress as Muhammad did. They try to repeat the special prayers he uttered upon going to sleep and waking up or even upon entering and leaving the bathroom.

As the last chapter showed, Islamic scholars have developed an enormous list of what to do and what not to do, and that raises the question of what happens to those who break some rules. Many Muslims are relaxed about that, content that daily ritual practices will cover over a multitude of sins. But some become frenzied when they break the rules, and there are so many to break. Some Muslims search for a "get out of jail free" card—if there is such a thing.

Those who have investigated the last days of the September 11 hijackers found that some took advantage of America's freedom to break lots of Quranic rules. On the day of their death, according to notebooks of two of the suicide-murderers, the plan was to "purify your heart and clean it from all earthly matters. The time of fun and waste has gone. . . . You have to be convinced that those few hours that are left you in your life are very few. From there you will begin to live the happy life, the infinite paradise." One fiery ending would purportedly pay for a multitude of sins.

Mainstream Islam has never considered self-martyrdom or kamikaze suicide a guarantor of immediate access to Paradise. Muslim jurists over the centuries have emphatically considered terrorist attacks against unsuspecting and defenseless victims to be immoral and downright evil. Arson and attacks against travelers also received harsh treatment, whatever the reason, and whether victims are Muslim or non-Muslim. Even if another country's attacks have created civilian casualties among Muslims, traditional Islam still does not justify terroristic acts because the injustice of others does not create a license to kill. Nor are historical grievances such as the Crusades supposed to justify revenge brutality nine centuries later.

And yet, while Muslims agree that it's not right to attack civilians or innocent bystanders, some are making up new definitions of noncombatant categories. Some Palestinian groups war on every Israeli, conveniently claiming that almost all citizens receive some military training so that few people are civilians and no one is innocent. It's only one step from that to claim that every Pentagon worker is an enemy because the U.S. supports Israel. It's one step further to declare everyone at the World Trade Center an enemy because capitalists control the world. It's a further step beyond to state, as bin Laden did in 1999 to *Newsweek,* that "any American who pays taxes to his government . . . is our target, because he is helping the American war machine against the Muslim nation."

At various times in Muslim history, factions arose that took extra steps down what can quickly become a slippery slope. The Kharajites became infamous within early Islam for murdering Muslims who disagreed with them. Centuries later, some Muslims who used hashish to get themselves ready to kill originated the word *assassin.* Orthodox Muslims saw these killers as evil, much as Ku Klux Klan members claim to be Christian or the Northern Ireland IRA or Serbian leadership's claims to be waging Christian holy war. Yet violent movements within Islam continue to arise, and it's worth asking whether particular elements of Islamic doctrine push some Muslims toward extremes.

One obvious element is a suspicion of diversity. For example, many Muslims wonder how the Bible could be an inspired work when many different authors produced it over a period of more than a thousand years. They look amiss at the story of Christ's life and death being given in four separate Gospels: If there are four separate accounts, they must all be false. The Quran, seen as having come through one mediator over twenty-three years, is much more credible.

Christianity is about the one and the many, monotheism with a trinity. Muslims see the tension in holding firmly to both, and they are right. That tension has pushed Christians to build a society that emphasizes both unity and diversity and in that way reflects the Trinity. The Muslim emphasis on *tawhid,* making everything united, has huge cultural implications. Abraham questioned God about the destruction of Sodom, but the word *Islam* means "submission," period. This carries over into a reluctance to accept the legitimacy of critics. Concerning intellectual liberty in Muslim countries, Hisham Kassem of the Egyptian Organization for Human Rights said, "It's not safe to think in this part of the world."

Although the Quran states that "there is no compulsion in religion," Islamic states often interpret that to mean that "there is no competition in religion" within their borders. Iraq, Iran, Syria, Saudi Arabia, Sudan, Pakistan, Indonesia, Kuwait, and Egypt are among the countries blasted by the State Department's year 2000 Report on International Religious Freedom. In hard-core Muslim countries, any Muslim who becomes a Christian may forfeit his life, family, or property. In several "moderate" Muslim countries, churches are allowed but Bibles and church bulletins must remain behind church walls.

The emphasis on unicity also has governmental implications. Without a sense of original sin, Lord Acton's idea that power corrupts and absolute power corrupts absolutely does not arise. A system of checks and balances seems redundant, and dictators abound. Originally Islamic countries had no separation between religious and civil law, between Islam and the state, and that is the way radical Muslims want things to be once again. According to this thinking, Islamic societies should not shape laws to fit their specific histories; they are to submit.

Because Islam in many ways trains people not to govern themselves but to be governed by dictates, Muslim countries almost always been run by dictators. Those rulers have had much in common with the rulers of Marxist countries. It's not surprising that Egypt, Syria, Iraq, Libya, and other countries in the 1960s turned away from the United States even though the United States successfully pressured British, French, and Israeli forces to withdraw from the Suez Canal in 1956. It's not surprising now that terrorists from Marxist remnants and radical Islam work well together.

Islam emphasizes a master-servant relationship between man and Allah that is different than the father-child relationship that exists between God and redeemed persons in Christianity. Fathers face conflicting impulses: Do you hug a child with a mild injury, or do you tell him to be a man? That leads to a creative tension between soft and hard in Christianity, a tension that comes out in the compassionate conservative goal of being tough-minded but tenderhearted. In Christian theology the tension between God's holiness and God's mercy is resolved through Christ's sacrifice. That tension does not exist within Islam's master-servant relationship.

Nor does Islam understand compassion—suffering with the poor—in the way that Christianity does. Jesus tasted hostility from men and knew what it was to be unjustly tortured and abandoned, to endure overwhelming loss, and to then be killed. Muhammad encountered opposition but died in his bed, with wives ministering to him. The ancient Greeks distinguished between *gnosis* (intellectual knowledge) and *epignosis,* intimate understanding. In Christianity, God has both kinds of knowledge concerning man's suffering and still invites us to draw near to him.

Columnist Peggy Noonan wrote about a husband and wife swimming in the ocean when "from nowhere came a shark. The shark went straight for the woman, opened its jaws. Do you know what the man did? He punched the shark in the head. . . . So the shark let go of his wife and went straight for him. And it killed him. The wife survived to tell the story of what her husband had done. He had tried to deck the shark." The Quran has no sense of a God who would become man and give his life to deck the shark. The idea is blasphemous to Muslims: If God becomes man, doesn't that lower God to man's level? Perhaps the woman had sinned and should be eaten by the shark. Or if she was innocent, Allah from on high could zap the shark.

In Christianity the church is the bride of Christ, who gave his life for her; husbands are to love their wives enough to die for them. The husband-wife relationship in Islam also mirrors its theology, which means marriage is in many ways a master-servant relationship. While the Quran calls husbands "guardians," some Muslims say that recalcitrant wives can be beaten, based on S 4:34: "As for those from whom you fear rebellion, admonish them and banish them to beds apart, and scourge them." Others say that only the lightest tap is allowed, but all agree that Muslim men can be polygamous, based loosely on the model of Muhammad; after his first wife died he married nine to thirteen other women, and one hadith claimed he had intercourse with nine of his wives on a single night.

Muslim men are to have a maximum of four wives; since unlimited polygamy was an option before the Quran, this is hailed as a notable advance. (One section of the Quran specifies that all the wives are to be treated equally, and another section says that is impossible, so some Muslims have argued that the Quran actually supports monogamy, but that is definitely a minority opinion.) Three Muslim justifications for polygamy are often advanced. When many men have been killed in wars, males are scarce. Polygamy is better than the Western custom of having mistresses or dumping old wives and garnering trophy wives. (Do American cultural embarrassments justify institutionalized humiliation?) The Muslim system is better than leaving a husband frustrated if a wife cannot have children. (But what about wives whose husbands are sterile?)

The husband supplies money or goods that remain in the wife's possession should he initiate a divorce. The husband has a unilateral right to do so by saying, "I divorce you" twice, waiting three menstrual cycles, and then saying it a third time: that finalizes the divorce, without any need of a court decree. (The waiting period is designed to make sure the woman is not pregnant, or if she is, to make clear the husband's paternity. It also allows a man to rethink his decision, while others try to mediate.) A man usually gains custody of boys over seven years old and girls over nine.

The Quran emphasizes modest dress for women, but it is only since the 1930s that Islamic dress, veil and all, has become common as a statement of Muslim orthodoxy. Women are not to draw attention to their beauty and are to wear some form of head covering; at the time of Muhammad, it was probably a loose scarf covering her head, neck, and shoulders; but it is often interpreted today as the complete *chador* covering. Such clothing is seen as leading to greater respect for Muslim women and less incitement of men to lust. Genital mutilation, although not in the Quran, is practiced on one in five Muslim girls; it is designed to keep women from lusting.

The Bible includes some hard laws that were designed to create a holy land; within Islam every land in which Muslims live is to be a holy land, and thus Quranic law must not be modified. One of Islam's best-known rules is that, according to the Quran and the hadith, the right hand of a thief is to be cut off, even if he makes restitution and pledges never to steal again. That's different from the Bible, which has a thief paying back what he has stolen and asking for forgiveness. (What has to be paid back depends on what he stole and whether he has already disposed of the item. The amount given in the Bible is 1.2, 2, 4, or 5 times what he stole, but never is he marred for life.)

Christianity is the religion of the second chance. With Islam it's often one strike and you're out. Jesus tells the woman caught in adultery, after he has shamed those who might have condemned her publicly, "Go and sin no more" (John 8:11 NKJV). One hadith tells about a woman pregnant by adultery coming to Muhammad: He has her treated decently until she gives birth and then has her stoned to death. Islam teaches that Allah loves the righteous, but

Christianity teaches that "while we were yet sinners, Christ died for us" (Rom. 5:8).

Is this hard religion inevitably an aggressive one? It's not hard to find bloody Quran verses. For instance, Sura 8:39, "And fight with them until there is no more persecution and religion should be only for Allah." Or 9:14, "Fight them, Allah will punish them by your hands and bring them to disgrace." Or 9:29, "Fight those who do not believe in Allah . . . until they pay the tax in acknowledgment of superiority and they are in a state of subjection." Islamic scholars in turn tend to point to exterminate-the-Canaanite passages in the book of Joshua or the order in 1 Samuel to commit genocide against the Amalekites, to which Jews and Christians reply that those writings reflect special circumstances, to which Muslims say, "So do ours."

Thrusts and parries can continue on those lines, but two pairs of facts are unarguable. First, Jesus was a man of peace; Muhammad at times was a man of war. Christians read the Old Testament's bloody passages in light of the New; Muslims have nothing to take the edge off. Second, Christianity initially spread through nonaggressive means, especially the blood of martyrs, while Islam initially spread at least in part through military conflict, with the blood of its opponents often flowing. Christianity held up its peaceful dead for imitation; Islam, its warlike victors.

It is also easy to find verses promising that good things will happen to all who die in a campaign to spread Islam. "Those who fly in Allah's way and are then slain or die," Sura 22:58 promises, "Allah will most certainly grant them a goodly sustenance, and most surely Allah is the best Giver of sustenance." Some of Muhammad's hadith sayings indicate that those who die fighting for Allah receive special benefits. Muslims such as the eleventh-century Persian philosopher Avicenna have suggested that spreading Islam by any means creates the greatest good for the greatest number in the life to come, and any suffering inflicted in this life is minor compared to the joy to come. That type of theological utilitarian thinking has contributed to a different sense of liberty than is common in the Western world.

Professor Mumtaz Ali Khan offers a typical statement: "Freedom of religion means the right of an individual to practice, profess and propagate his religion . . . . Freedom of expression means the liberty that every individual has to convey his thoughts. . . . But he should not express his views in a manner that offends the feelings of the general community to which he belongs."

In that environment Salman Rushdie had to hide to preserve his life, and a host of other critics of Islam have been shot or knifed. Khan wrote about Rushdie, "He could easily be called a perverted scholar. Being a Muslim, what forced him to resort to character assassination of the Holy Prophet Muhammad? . . . There was absolutely no need for him to bring in the holy Prophet and his wife in the story. But his poisonous mind could not rest in peace unless he wrote something to suit and justify his temperament. None can pardon him after reading the book."

Few Muslims could pardon former Southern Baptist Convention president Jerry Vines after he, in the summer of

2002, attacked Muhammad for (according to some *hadith*) marrying a six-year-old and having sexual relations with her at age nine. Since the *New York Times* swung on Vines for engaging in "hate speech against Muslims," I wrote a column defending Vines's right to bring up that piece of information, noting that it came right out of Muslim sources. Dr. Aslam Abdallah, editor of *Minaret,* a major Muslim monthly magazine published in Los Angeles, then asked me, "Where did you get the information that Muhammad married a six-year-old girl?" I told him that it came from hadith collected by Sahih Bukhari, Sahih Muslim, and Sunan Dawud over a thousand years ago, and I gave him the page numbers.

I thought that would end the matter, but Abdallah replied, "Muslim scholars have refuted these hadith and questioned their authenticity." That was interesting, I responded, because Bukhari is "considered the most authentic of all the hadith authors/editors. If what he writes is not authentic, don't you have to throw out a lot of the Islamic tradition?" Abdallah replied that "any hadith that contradicts the Quran is not reliable." Since the Quran opposes adults having sexual relations with children, and since the Quran states that Muhammad was sinless, any hadith to the contrary must be tossed aside.

In the fall of 2002, Muslim anger about purported disrespect to Muhammad led to Nigerian riots that left 220 persons dead and more than 1,000 seriously injured, with numerous churches burned to the ground. As *Los Angeles Times* correspondent Davan Maharaj reported, "Thousands of Muslim youths armed with knives and machetes [were] burning cars and assaulting bystanders they suspected were Christian. Rioters pulled a local journalist off a motorcycle and told him he would be killed unless he could recite verses from Islam's holy book, the Quran. The crowd released him unharmed when they realized he was Muslim."

Christian fundamentalists did not act that way when writers depicted Jesus as a homosexual or when an artist submerged a cross in urine. But the offending party in this instance was a writer for the Nigerian newspaper *ThisDay* who, musing on how Muhammad would react to the Miss World beauty pageant, stated that "he would have probably chosen a wife from one of them." That's a reasonable speculation, given that hadith show Muhammad appreciating and sometimes appropriating to himself the beauties of his time. Book eight, numbers 3325 and 3328, of the sayings and deeds collected by the esteemed ninth-century editor Abul Husain Muslim bin al-Hajjaj al-Nisapuri, records how Muhammad heard that a young woman was so beautiful that a disciple said, "She is worthy of you only." Muhammad had her brought to him and was so enraptured that he "granted her emancipation and married her."

What is the insecurity that leaves so many Muslims ready to riot at the drop of a historically accurate assessment? Could it be that Islam has been on an international losing streak during the past several centuries? If so, were terrorists hailed simply because they struck a blow against a powerful country, and if they had been allowed to get away with it, would more blows have quickly come? That's why scholar David Forte contended after September 11, "If we have respect for ourselves, if we have respect for Islam, we can no longer tolerate the evil they [the terrorists] represent. Two civilizations hang in the balance."

The concept of inalienable rights is a starting point for understanding one more key difference between Bible-based and Islamic civilizations. As John Ashcroft put it in his celebrated and maligned speech at Bob Jones University, "We knew that we were endowed not by the king, but by the Creator, with certain inalienable rights. If America is to be great in the future, it will be if we understand that our source is not civic and temporal, but our source is godly and eternal: Endowed by the Creator with rights of life, liberty and the pursuit if happiness."

Such talk of "inalienable rights" may sound like boilerplate rhetoric, but it is crucial in differentiating Christian and Islamic political philosophy. As the pioneering historian Bat Ye'Or has pointed out in *The Dhimmi* and her other remarkable books over the past two decades, Islam has no belief in "inalienable rights." Instead Islam establishes rights for Muslims but gives Jews and Christians living in Muslim-ruled lands a special status as *dhimmis* (Arabic for "protected people").

The word *dhimmi* became historically significant in AD 628 when Muhammad's forces defeated a Jewish tribe that lived at the oasis of Khaybar and made with them a treaty known as the *dhimma*. The treaty allowed Jews to continue cultivating their oasis as long as they gave Muhammad half of their produce. Crucially Muhammad reserved the right to break the deal and expel the Jews whenever he wished. That agreement has served as a model for Muslims over the centuries.

Dhimmis typically had to pay discriminatory taxes acknowledging publicly their status as second-class citizens. They were on the hook for additional sums payable on Islamic demand. They had to supply forced labor on demand. They were ineligible for any public office and without the right even to testify in legal battles. They were not allowed to construct new places of worship but some- times received permission to worship in buildings that pre- date Muslim conquest. (The buildings had to be dilapidated, with no crosses or bell ringing allowed, and Muslims were able to ransack them at will.)

Dhimmis were not allowed to possess weapons, marry Muslim women, meet with others on the streets, or ride horse or camels (the two "noble animals"). *Dhimmis* had to wear special clothes, walk with eyes lowered, and accept being pushed aside by Muslims. *Dhimmis* had to have low doors on their houses; they could have no lights on the doors. Some particular aspects varied from age to age and region to region. In the ninth century Jews in some Muslim areas had to wear on their shoulders a patch of white cloth that bore the image of an ape; Christians, since they ate pork, wore a pig image. In the eleventh century Seville Jews could not be met with the greeting, "Peace be unto you," because they were not supposed to have any peace.

The Muslim goal in collecting taxes from *dhimmis* was to maximize not only revenue but abuse. North African nineteenth-century theologian al-Maghali advised that *dhimmis* be assembled on tax day "in the lowest and dirtiest place," with threatening officials placed above the *dhimmis* "so that it seems to them, as well as to the others, that our object is to degrade them." With the stage set, al-Maghali advised, officials could play out a little drama of dragging *dhimmis* "one by one (to the official responsible) for the exacting of payment." They would knock him around, then thrust him aside, and make sure he realized that his position would never improve. As al-Maghali put it, "This is the way that the friends of the Lord, of the first and last generations will act toward their infidel enemies, for might belongs to Allah, to His Prophet, and to the Believers."

Other edicts affected not just finances but self-respect. A Cairo rule in 1761 was that "no Jew or Christian may appear on horseback. They ride only asses, and must alight upon meeting even the lowest Egyptian lord. . . . If the infidel fails to give instant obedience, he is beaten." In Persia in 1890, Jewish women have to "expose their faces in public [like prostitutes]. . . . The men must not wear fine clothes, the only material permitted them being a blue cotton fabric. They are forbidden to wear matching shoes. Every Jew is obliged to wear a piece of red cloth on his chest. A Jew must never overtake a Muslim on a public street. . . . If a Muslim insults a Jew, the latter must drop his head and remain silent. . . . The Jew cannot put on his coat; he must be satisfied to carry it rolled under his arm. . . . It is forbidden for Jews to leave the town or enjoy the fresh air of the countryside. . . . Jews must not consume good fruit."

Muslims showed great patience in psychologically weakening their opponents. For example, authorities would allow bells inside churches but not outside, anticipating that the bells inside would "eventually fall into disuse. For the bells are normally attached to the church steeple so that when rung they may be heard from afar. If they are obliged to ring them within the church, then no one will hear them or pay heed to them and they will be abolished altogether since they will serve no purpose." The result of beating and belittlement was obvious to observers in Turkey two centuries ago, who noted that *dhimmis* have "the most submissive cringing tone," and in Morocco during the 1870s, who said Jews had terrorized expressions.

Should that be surprising? Didn't Jews have terrorized expressions in Christian-ruled territories? Bat Ye'or argues that "dhimmitude is in no way comparable with the position of Jews in Christendom." Jews in Europe were an oppressed minority; Christians and Jews in many Muslim countries were oppressed majorities. Persecution of a majority is no different ethically than persecution of a minority, but it requires establishment of a police state rather than just use of the police. "The realm of dhimmitude," Bat Ye'or writes, "is actually situated in a political ideology of permanent war which ruined entire regions, justified massacres, slavery, usurpation of land, and deportations."

French philosopher Jacques Ellul, in an introduction to Bat Ye'or's *The Dhimmi,* also differentiated the situation of the dhimmi from that of the European serf in the Middle Ages. Serfdom, he noted, "was the result of certain historical changes such as the transformation of slavery . . . when these historical conditions altered, the situation of the serf also evolved until his status finally disappeared." *Dhimmi* status, though, "was not the product of the historical accident but . . . the expression of an absolute, unchanging, theologically grounded Muslim conception of the relationship between Islam and non-Islam. It is not a historical accident of retrospective interest, but a necessary condition of existence."

What are the necessary conditions of existence within an Islamic worldview? Muslims, like Christians, divide people into believers and non-believers, but the Islamic conception of future relations between the two is different. Christians believe that final Christian victory will come not primarily through the efforts of Christians but only when Christ returns. For Muslims, though, the world is divided into the *dar al-Harb,* land controlled by non-Muslims that forms the "territory of war," and the *dar al-Islam,* the land where Islamic law prevails. This is a permanent state of war, although there may be truces, because it is man's might that will make Islam supreme throughout the world.

In Islam, therefore, a peace is not a peace, and a truce should not last longer than ten years. A time of peace longer than a decade is occasion not for relaxation but for feeling inadequate and fidgety. Infidels should never be allowed to rest on their laurels, famed fourteenth-century Muslim jurist Ibn Taymiyya asserted; any land they possess is held illegitimately. This means that jihad is not aggression but retrieving what is Islam's legitimate possession. The *dar al-Harb* has no right to exist.

Muslims have long understood the difference between the Islamic and Christian agendas and the way that Muslim centralism can contribute to a mission of permanent war. Medieval philosopher Ibn Khaldun wrote:

In the Muslim community, the holy war is a religious duty, because of the universalism of the [Muslim] mission and the obligation to convert everyone to Islam either by persuasion or by force. Therefore, caliphate and royal authority are united [in Islam], so that the person in charge can devote the available strength to both of them [religion and politics] at the same time. The other religious groups did not have a universal mission, and the holy war was not a religious duty to them, save only for purposes of defense.

If Bat Ye'or is right, we should speak about the Muslim assignment of *dhimmi* status not only in the past tense but in the present and future tenses as well. As Ellul wrote, "Because of Islam's fixed ideological mode. . . . One must know as exactly as possible what the Muslims did with these unconverted conquered peoples, because that is what they will do in the future (and are doing right now)." Based on the experience of Christians in Sudan and Indonesia, Ellul's pessimistic realism is well warranted. Dhimmitude is not merely something to be studied by historians; it still goes on wherever Islam gains an edge.

Today it's hard to find a Christian who says slavery was righteous because slaves were kept alive. Muslims defend dhimmitude, however, by saying that Muslims could have expelled or killed Christians and Jews but deserve credit for letting them live. (Of course, genocide against the inhabitants of conquered nations would have left Arabs with depopulated areas and not much likelihood of repopulating them.) Some also have praised Islam for giving opportunities to the children of *dhimmis*. (Muslims often removed children from their Christian or Jewish parents and brought them up in Islam. That went along with the belief that all children are born Muslims, or some corrupted by parents.)

Other defenders of Islam have asserted that *dhimmi* status was better than anything offered Jews prior to Islamic conquest. Christianity. That is generally not true: for example, under Byzantine authority Jews could not purchase any property that the church had; under Islam, they could purchase no property, period. Under the Byzantines, Jews could act as witnesses; not so under Islam. But in any event, those who accepted *dhimmi* status, Bat Ye'or notes, were left with "no genuine rights," because "the person who concedes the charter can equally well rescind it. . . . Under dhimmitude, a person has no claim to any rights, just permission that can be rescinded. This is not because of temporary decision but is a rooted concept."

In short, Quranic and biblical political philosophy are worlds apart. Orthodox Jews and Christians may be nice people, and they can also live at peace with their neighbors, since all people have inalienable rights. Orthodox Muslims may be nice people, but to remain faithful to Quranic teaching they can only have a temporary cease-fire with *dhimmis*.

This is a huge difference that many journalists have irresponsibly overlooked.

Islam Time Line

610 Muhammad rejects both Christianity and Judaism and begins to develop his own monotheistic religion.

622 Muhammad flees Mecca. This becomes year 1 in the Muslim calendar. Over the next ten years he succeeds as both teacher and general.

632 Muhammad dies without a clear political heir; Muslim infighting begins.

637 Muslims capture Jerusalem and soon possess Egypt, Syria, Mesopotamia, Persia, Cyprus, Tripoli, and Afghanistan.

661 At the end of a Muslim civil war, Muhammad's nephew Ali is murdered, and the Sunni-Shiite division begins.

700 Muslims, sweeping across North Africa and virtually wiping out Christianity there, conquer Algiers.

711 Muslims conquer most of Spain.

732 Muslims are defeated at Tours/Poitiers in what is now Southern France; they conquer little more of Western Europe.

786 Harun al-Rashid, Caliph in Baghdad, leads the way toward a golden age of Muslim learning.

846 Muslims sack Rome and the Vatican; meanwhile, mathematician and geographer al-Khwarazmi (algorithm is derived from his name) advances knowledge.

900 The writing of *1001 Arabian Nights* begins, and the Arab physician Rhases becomes the first to describe smallpox, plague, and other infectious diseases.

963 Al Sufi's *Book of Fixed Stars,* which mentions nebula, is one indication of Muslim superiority in astronomy.

1006 Muslims settle in Northwest India.

1037 Ibn Sina (Avicenna), the most influential Islamic medieval philosopher/physician, dies.

1094 El Cid defeats Muslims in Spain.

1095 Pope Urban II calls for a Crusade.

1099 Crusaders capture and sack Jerusalem.

1187 Muslims under Saladin retake Jerusalem.

1250 First Muslim states in Southeast Asia are developing.

1380 Ottoman Empire emerges.

1453 Muslims capture Constantinople, renaming it Istanbul, and turn St. Sophia Basilica into a mosque.

1492 Muslim governments, gradually pushed back for centuries, lose their last toehold in Spain.

1529 Muslims besiege Vienna but do not take it.

1571 Battle of Lepanto ends Muslim naval power in the Mediterranean.

1654 Taj Mahal completed.

1669 Muslim rulers in India prohibit Hindu worship.

1683 Muslims besiege Vienna, again unsuccessfully, but over the years control big chunks of Southeastern Europe.

1792 Ibn Abdul Wahhab, founder of the radical Islamic movement known as Wahhabism, dies.

1816 British bombard Algiers and force its ruler to end the enslavement of Christians.

1869 The Tunisian government, in debt, accepts European financial control, in one of many changes throughout the century that resulted in North Africa falling under the control of France, England, and Italy.

1918 Ottoman Empire, allied with Germany, collapses.

1928 The radical Muslim Brotherhood is founded in Egypt.

1947 England relinquishes control of India, which is partitioned into Hindu India and Muslim Pakistan.

1948 England relinquishes control of Palestine, which is partitioned into Jewish and Muslim states.

1967 Israel defeats Arab armies and takes control over the West Bank and the Gaza Strip.

1979 Muslim radicals take over Iran.

1991 U.S. and allies rout Iraqi army.

2001 Almost three thousand die in the September 11 attack on the United States.

2003 Muslim respect for American power increases as U.S. quickly defeats Iraq, but guerrilla war continues.

Chapter Nine
Missing the Story

In the face of Hitler's aggression in 1940, John F. Kennedy wrote a provocatively titled book, *Why England Slept*. The September 11 attacks woke up the U.S. in 2001, but the tendency in democracies is to take naps whenever the coast is temporarily clear. Many people who enjoy reading morning newspapers while sipping their coffee would be surprised to find the papers acting as sleeping pills when it comes to covering not only Islam but other religions.

Such pills can be fatal because the world is a dangerous place. Not only Islam displays militaristic tendencies. Thinking of Gandhi, we often view Hindus as pacifists, but the *Bhagavad Gita*, Hinduism's favorite scripture, is a wonderful poem with many themes: one prominent one is an endorsement of not only war but war against relatives. Hindu militants today speak loudly and wave big sticks, including nuclear ones. Buddhism also is not necessarily a religion of peace, as the records of Buddhist forces that dominated medieval Japan show. New documentation shows how Zen Buddhist thought underlay Japan's buildup to an attack on Pearl Harbor.

U.S. journalists typically are not familiar with such militancy, but those at major media outlets do tend to be militant in one respect. As Don Feder (an Orthodox Jewish syndicated columnist) has noted, they are often "militant modernists. They view faith as primitive and the Bible as charming poetry but certainly not anything to be taken seriously. They can no more conceive of basing a moral judgment on a religious principle than of basing an investment decision on the phases of the moon."

Today only about one in ten reporters and editors at leading publications attend religious services weekly (compared to four in ten among the general population). Most of the journalists who do attend choose theologically liberal, loose constructionist churches or synagogues where they are also unlikely to hear about biblical reasons for thinking or acting in particular ways. In practice, many leading news publications and their reporters tend to pay little attention to religion, unless there is scandal. It takes someone who cares about religions to spend time studying their sacred writings and working at theological knots until some understanding is reached.

For example, to grasp Islam, it is vital to understand what *jihad* means within the religion, and to do that takes some work. To grasp Buddhism, the nonattachment principle must be studied. To grasp Hinduism, journalists must be willing to delve into the implications of believing in karma and the transmigration of souls. It is often necessary to wrestle from dusk to dawn to develop some understanding, and those who think religion unimportant, are likely to give up quickly.

Two s-words characterize the normal U.S. newspaper coverage of the four religions we've looked at in this book: *superficiality* and *syncretism,* the attempt to merge religions under the assumption that they are all basically the same. Using the Lexis-Nexis data base, my students and I have looked at thousands of articles from the past several years; below are a few excerpts that suggest the whole. (Readers who wish to read the entire articles may hop on Lexis-Nexis and access them by inserting the phrases quoted.)

Coverage of Judaism

Judaism was the first major religion truly to concentrate on things unseen, and that represents a problem for newspapers that focus on what can be seen and touched. The problem was evident in an *Austin American-Statesman* article that emphasized the ritual of Torah scrolls being walked from one synagogue building to a new sanctuary. "'It's heavy,' said Diane Radin as she carried one of the larger scrolls," but the reporter provided no sense of the real weight of Scripture. She described each of the six scrolls but mentioned nothing about their contents.

Similarly, the *American-Statesman* article about Rosh Hashana, the Jewish New Year's Day, did not note that Rosh Hashana is *yom ha'din,* "the day of judgment," the day Jews believe God decides which names will be in the "book of life" and which in the "book of death" for the coming year. Editors who took such matters seriously might think this was "news you can use," news so significant that it is announced by the blowing of a shofar, a ram's horn. But instead of reporting that news, the *American-Statesman* covered the making of shofars.

Readers could learn about how the shofar "needs to be washed, sawed, drilled, sanded, washed again, and varnished." Readers could follow the whole process and then cut out a 350-word sidebar on "how to make your own shofar." Readers would not learn, though, what the blowing of the shofar announced. What they got was the equivalent of a story about the Super Bowl that dealt only with the singing of the National Anthem.

The period between Rosh Hashana and the end of Yom Kippur ten days later is called the Ten Days of Repentance because the Talmud suggests that a person's behavior during that period might lead God to alter a tough call. An *American-Statesman* article mentioned that "on Yom Kippur, Jews believe God will pass judgment on them," and then emphasized the performance: "Cantors, like celebrated opera stars, prepare and deliver the prayers wrapped in ancient melodies with an individual style. . . . It can be an exhausting experience, but they say the meaning of the prayers feeds the soul. Still, the body can become tired."

Stories about Yom Kippur in other newspapers were similarly superficial. The *San Antonio Express-News* headlined one story "The Ancient Power of Yom Kippur" and noted that "synagogues will be full. Before sundown, congregants will listen to the emotional tones of the chanted Kol Nidre. . . . 'It's an overwhelming experience, coming together with the whole community, all of us bringing our failures with us.

When you hear that music, it stirs your soul,' [Cantor David] Silverstein said."

Newspapers typically looked with favor on those trying to syncretize Judaism and Buddhism. Under the headline "'Buddhist Translation of Biblical Psalms," the *San Francisco Chronicle* ran a gushing profile of Norman Fischer, who "was born a Jew and grew up chanting the Psalms in Hebrew" but did not like to think of God destroying his enemies. Mr. Fischer became a Buddhist and wrote *Opening to You: Zen-Inspired Translations of the Psalms,* in which words such as *God* or *Lord* are "usually just replaced by the word You, a simple trick that allows the reader to find whatever Higher Power floats his or her boat."

The article concluded, "Some conservative Christians or Orthodox Jews might find blasphemy in *Opening to You,* but Fischer's inspired revision of these ancient poems will enable many others to see old Scripture in a new light." The *Chronicle* also profiled Jack Kornfeld, another convert from Judaism to Buddhism, and described how he was taking "his 18-year-old daughter to a Yom Kippur service in a San Geronimo Valley community center. . . . Someone asked her what her religion was and she said, 'Jewish Buddhist Hindu Christian.'"

Curiously, those who combined two religions that do have many overlaps, Judaism and Christianity, tended to receive mostly critical attention. The *Florida Times-Union* (Jacksonville) headlined one story, "Messianic Jews Find Faith in Blend," but started and ended with the implication that the blend did not work. The story began, "Rabbi Bob

Cohen has seen the dirty looks when he shows up at Jewish celebrations. He and other Messianic Jews have heard the barbs from those who call their religion a sham, a disgrace, and a back-door ploy by Christians to convert Jews."

After a brief explanation—"Unlike traditional Judaism, Messianic Judaism also follows the teaching of the New Testament and recognizes Jesus Christ as the Messiah"—came the type of scornful quotation that rarely appears in an article about theological liberals: "'People who say "my Judaism is fulfilled by Jesus Christ" are trying to play football with bats,' said Rabbi Eliezer Ben-Yehuda of Ponte Vedra Beach, who also denounces Cohen's title of rabbi." The article did include some statistics—"about 250 Messianic synagogues have been established across the country"—followed by another hostile statement: "'We call them Hebrew Christians,' Jews for Judaism Director Mark Powers said of Messianic Jews. 'It's a fraud. It's Christianity dressed in Jewish clothing.'"

The *Times-Union* also included description of and quotation from adherents: "About 150 people attended a recent Friday service at Beth Jacob. Several men wore yarmulkes; some women wore mesh scarves on their heads. Some carried Bibles titled Complete Jewish Bible that included both testaments. . . . Arlene Yahre of Orange Park was raised Jewish, but said observing Jewish laws didn't make her feel connected to God. 'I don't feel I need all those rituals. They keep you busy, busy, busy. They cloud things,' said Yahre, who adopted the Messianic faith about two years ago." But the story ended with a quotation whose equivalent is not seen in stories regarding feminist or gay religious adherents: "Yahre said she wishes people would understand Messianic Jews better. 'We're not so far out nutso,' she said."

The *New York Times* gave disproportionate coverage to the activities of theologically liberal groups. For example, the *Times* in 2001, under the headline "Humanist Jewish Group Reaches New Milestone," reported that "two years ago, an organization of secular humanist Jews celebrated a milestone, the first ordination of a rabbi trained within their movement. Last night, the group took another step forward, ordaining three more at a temple outside Detroit." The writer later revealed that a not-so-grand total of six other students were being trained by the Society for Humanistic Judaism. How often does the internationally renowned *Times* deign to spend its highly sought-after space on a tiny organization?

Journalists regularly led cheers for the Jewish left even in conservative towns like Salt Lake City, where the *Salt Lake Tribune* gave little attention to an existing Orthodox synagogue in order to herald what its headline called a "Jewish Blossoming; New Park City rabbi balances progressive thinking with Jewish tradition." The writer told of how "Rabbi Joshua Aaronson goes to work in a golf shirt, but not a yarmulke," and then quoted the rabbi's desire "to establish the most creative, innovative, and open Jewish community in North America. . . . I want our children to know that whomever they decide to embrace as a life-partner—a Jew, a non-Jew, a person of the same sex or a person of the opposite sex—there will be a place for them in this community."

Some newspapers even pretended that the controversy within Judaism about "gay marriage" within Judaism doesn't even exist. *The Ledger* (Lakeland, Fla.) headlined one story, "Reform Rabbi Weighs Uniting Same-sex Couples," and did not follow the typical newspaper practice of displaying (if not provoking) dispute. The article quoted the rabbi's willingness to officiate at gay weddings because "just as the rabbis of old made changes in their understanding of the Bible to meet the knowledge of the day, rabbis of today can do no less." *The Ledger* did not quote anyone in opposition.

We cannot and should not expect newspapers to concentrate on things unseen, but they should report what can readily be seen: the concentration of Orthodox Jews on the state of their souls and not the skill of the shofar player and the differences between Reform and Orthodox Jews on issues such as homosexuality. The natural American journalistic tendency is to chase controversy, so in one sense the tough Jacksonville coverage of the Messianic Jewish controversy is a good sign—if only reporters would do the same with other groups. When journalists ignore opportunities for feisty debate, the fix is in.

Coverage of Hinduism

As we have seen, at a popular level Hindus bow to what temples unabashedly call idols, but at an intellectual level Hindus are worshipping Brahman, the supreme god, the impersonal ultimate reality, the world soul. Many Hindus assert that man, animals, and god are essentially the same since the universe is one unitary, organic whole with no independent parts. They say people and animals at some point appear to be separate from God and that we even think the split natural. They say we will find no true, lasting happiness until we lose our individuality by becoming reabsorbed into the cosmic whole from which we came.

How do American journalists even begin to explain, in the context of a feature story, something so complicated? Can they at least give a sense of complexity and nuance? That's vital for the education of readers and also crucial for future relations between India, one of the world's nuclear powers, and the United States. India gained its independence partly through the work of Mahatma Gandhi, but India's current leaders do not hold to his pacifism either internationally—regularly threatening war against Pakistan—or domestically.

The domestic danger gained some publicity early in 2003 as Human Rights Watch (HRW) slammed Hindu groups for leading riots against Muslims and also noted attacks on Christians generally and the lynching of lower-caste members in particular. Earlier HRW had noted dozens of Hindu-led attacks against Christians, some ending in murder, and many condoned by India's ruling political party, Bharatiya Janata. HRW in 1999 reported that three Hindu groups were responsible for "the killings of priests, the raping of nuns, and the physical destruction of Christian institutions, schools, churches, colleges, and cemeteries. Thousands of Christians have also been forced to convert to Hinduism."

One incident that received some press coverage culminated in the burning to death in 1999 of Australian missionary Graham Staines and his two sons as they slept in their jeep in Eastern India. Many Hindu leaders criticized such attacks, but others justified them by saying that missionaries who preach "that the only way to salvation is through Christ" deserve to be punished. Without much coverage, attacks go on. The *Pittsburgh Post-Gazette* covered one in January 2003, but only because a missionary from Pittsburgh came under attack from a Hindu mob wielding clubs and swords.

Journalists looking for contradictions should be swarming over Hinduism's alternating pacifism and militancy. The Hindu principle of *ahimsa* means that Hindus are not to harm any creatures; some extreme Hindus may even wear a cloth over their mouths to prevent the possible killing of small insects. How does that accord with terrorizing missionaries? Sadly, U.S. newspaper coverage of Hinduism displayed superficiality and syncretism.

Reporters typically treated Hinduism not like a mighty religion that can hold its own against critics but as a pet capable only of receiving pats on the head. Central Texas newspaper readers learn that "the Shree Raseshwari Radha Rani Temple rises from the Hill Country terrain like a giant Faberge egg" and that it is a place of "peace, harmony, and devotion to God." (Which god? No indication.) Journalists teach that "Hindus see no need for an intermediary or a prophet to come between humans and God. Hindus seek truth, and they practice nonviolence." (Which god? What do Hindus mean by "truth"? No indication.)

Reporters rarely asked basic questions about what Hindus believe happens after death. One story read,

"Members of the Hindu Temple of San Antonio prayed Wednesday for the soul of an American-born swami . . . asking that the swami's soul be granted eternal peace in God's presence." (But the Hindu goal is the achievement of *moksha*, generally seen as the extinction of personality.) Another reporter related, "Hindus believe that the soul never dies and reincarnation enables one to complete a journey to Nirvana, a oneness with God." (That "oneness" is not togetherness but the obliteration of individuality.)

The *Los Angeles Times* rarely prints testimonials to Christianity, but the newspaper gave space for one Hindu devotee to report "an 'incredible peace and an ability to deal with the toughest situations in business and not be swept away by it.'" The *Orlando Sentinel* told of how "Hindu spirituality encourages . . . a human being to achieve his or her highest potential. Ultimately all paths lead to the goal of self-realization." Those boilerplate sentiments led to a concluding sentence as to how "self-realization leads the way to Nirvana, which literally means extinguishing of desires." (How is that the highest potential? Doesn't that last sentence extinguish everything that precedes it?)

Reporters regularly erred in defining not only *moksha* but *karma*, using it as a synonym for good or bad fortune rather than an exact measure of what an individual deserves, based on what his current and previous incarnations achieved. The *Orlando Sentinel* began one story with the theologically illiterate statement that "the developers of Orlando's Hindu University of America are certain of one thing: The unique institution they are planning already has plenty of good karma." (Organizations do not have karma, and in any event it's impossible to be sure whether anyone has good karma except by seeing what happens to him day by day.)

The *Austin American-Statesman* also displayed theological ignorance when it began a story, "After she showers and before she eats breakfast, Lalima Pathak chants and sings before the Hindu gods and goddesses that adorn the puja, or altar, in her dining room. . . . 'When I enter, I say, "Thank you for getting me home safe," and when I leave, I take a look at the puja and seek God's blessings to watch over me,' Pathak said." (Questions: With a broad variety of gods and goddesses, what does it mean for Hindus to seek capital-G "God's blessing"? And what difference would a blessing make anyway, since everything is determined by karma? Besides, *puja* is an activity, not an altar: Hindus do *puja*.)

Journalists normally are skeptical about leaders who foster unthinking obedience. The *Los Angeles Times,* though, offered a headline, "Hindus Flock to Temple to Meet Spiritual Leader," and waxed enthusiastic about how they began arriving at the Swaminarayan Hindu temple in Whittier at 6:30 a.m., as the waking sun broke through the morning mist. Thousands of Indian devotees from San Diego to Seattle, from Orange County to Oregon, flocked to the temple Sunday for the rare chance to see their spiritual leader, Pramukh Swami Maharaj. . . . Mrudula Dashi of La Verne watched enraptured by his faith. "For us, he is everything. For us, he's like a god."

Other laud followed: "'He's like a mountain of magnetism, and everyone is attracted to that,' she said." At this point journalistic warning lights should have been flashing as police lights do at an accident scene, but this reverential report continued: "What does this gentle old man in the saffron robe mean to the Hindu community? For the Swaminarayans . . . Pramukh Swami is the manifestation of God on Earth. 'How do you describe something so divine?' asked one follower. 'This is a lifetime memory,' said Rakesh Patel, a pharmacist who works in Long Beach and is also the temple spokesman. 'When you're with him, you can feel that he is divine. You think you know who you are, but he looks at your soul. You feel the presence of God.'"

The *Los Angeles Times'* unadulterated praise was also surprising because these Hindus "follow a puritanical path that preaches against drugs, alcohol, and television. To guard against illicit relations between the sexes, men and women are separated during worship. And women are forbidden from speaking to Pramukh Swami. All followers adhere to a strict vegetarian diet that prohibits even onions and garlic." A Christian "puritanical" group that made women second-class devotees would never receive such a positive story.

Many stories also expressed syncretism. The *San Antonio Express-News* summarized the message of Sri Viswayogi Viswamji, a visiting Hindu guru: "love, truth, peace, and eternal consciousness. . . . All the religions start with the same truth and are meant to show the divinity of God. . . . All religions start with the same truth and are meant to show the divinity of humanity." The first statement about all religions is arguable; the second is obviously wrong since all religions do not attempt to show humanity's "divinity," but in a medium that often searches for controversy the *Express-News* passed up the opportunity to have a debate.

Reporters regularly were conduits for swami syncretists, such as the one in Rhode Island who was prepared to respond to a request from one adherent "that Swami help him break free from all material attractions and ultimately take him to Akshardsham, the place 'you English-speaking people call Heaven.'" Journalists did not challenge those who "fell in love with Christ" at a Hindu-American ashram or said, "I consider myself a Christian, and what I find here at Kashi is all the principles I was taught" in church. The leader of that ashram exclaimed, "I love Jesus Christ."

The *Los Angeles Times* admiringly reported Hindu statements that "all faiths were essentially different paths to the same God, and in particular taught that an essential unity exists between original yoga and original Christianity—one reason that Jesus Christ is considered one of the gurus." The *Washington Post* even suggested that Christians should not cause pain to Hindus who are wounded by "the assertion by some Christians that Hindus 'are sinners' because they don't profess a belief in Jesus as savior and instead worship thousands of divine manifestations of God."

Similarly, the *Orlando Sentinel* journalist proclaimed, "Hinduism recognizes that there is one Truth, perceived and expressed by different people in different ways. This liberal view of God and humanity's relationship with God leads to an incomparable freedom of worship, and an acceptance of all ways of religious and spiritual inquiry." The unasked question: Why are Hindus and Muslims at each others' throats? Given press reports that Islam is a peace-loving religion, Muslims must not be causing problems, and Hindus are accepting of all, so the disputes are mysterious.

Coverage of Buddhism

As chapter 5 showed, Buddhists teach an attractive-sounding doctrine that has stunning implications for human interaction. Buddhism's top selling point is nonattachment to anything in the world; that, Gautama Buddha taught twenty-five hundred years ago, is the way to eliminate suffering. We shouldn't be emotionally attached to our houses or cars, our cats and dogs, our own health, or even (and here is where some who understand Buddhism drop out) our husbands or wives.

U.S. journalists, though, regularly portray Buddhism as merely an attack on selfishness. The *Kansas City Star* in 2001 reported this central Buddhist message: "We are most attached to our self-image. Friends are those who reinforce our image, and our enemies challenge it. In renouncing attachment to our self-image, we discover the truth about ourselves. . . . This leads to compassion for others and our own freedom." The opportunity for nonattachment to promote a lack of compassion ("don't mess up my tranquility") is rarely examined in articles that tend to be superficial and syncretistic.

For example, the *Dallas Morning News,* under a headline, "Buddhist Master Enthralls Devotees," printed Buddhist testimonies: "Lid Juarez found something four years ago that transformed his life. The 70-year-old Dallas man has lost

25 pounds, and chronic problems with indigestion and arthritis are gone. He said the hassles of day-to-day life no longer bother him, and he feels at peace 24 hours a day."

The *Deseret News* (Salt Lake City) provided a local Zen center an article that reads like an ad: "The center at 1274 E. South Temple continues to attract an increasing number of Utahns looking for a place to do some self-examination and find peace, . . . honesty, openness, love, and compassion."

Similarly, the *Austin American-Statesman* quoted Austin residents rejoicing that "Buddhism is very practical. Every day in your life you can use it and share. I feel very free and very content. Above all, I now discover the joy of life." The *San Francisco Chronicle* described Buddhism as nice-nice belief: "a philosophy that stresses the interconnectedness of life, and the importance of being kind to others." Writer Don Lattin had one convert to Buddhism explain that her mother at first was unhappy but is now pleased because the convert's "kids are kind to other kids."

Many Buddhist sects have arguments with one another that go back centuries, but U.S. newspapers almost never report those differences. One *St. Louis Post-Dispatch* article did note the existence of one division, but gave no detail about the differences, and then explained how representatives from each group eat together: "Everyone always loves the delicious vegetarian lunch." Political reporters do not overlook battles between U.S. solons because they eat bean soup together in the Senate dining room.

For example, one Buddhist sect, Soka Gakkai, has garnered wide criticism in Japan for its totalitarian nature and its control of the third largest political party in Japan. But a *Washington Post* article merely noted that "chanting is one of the features that distinguishes Soka Gakkai from better-known traditions that emphasize meditation." It then quoted one Soka Gakkai member, "While doing inner transformation, also at the same time you make efforts to transform society around you as a private citizen and collectively as a member of SGI." Sounds good.

Reporters regularly overlooked controversy and held out clichés as profundities. The *Denver Post* advised its readers through this headline: "Slow down, says Buddhist leader: Learn how to see 'beauty everywhere.'" A novel idea, and there was more from the teaching of Thich Nhat Hanh: "'Pay attention to the world in which you live. . . . The seeds for happiness are everywhere—in the blue sky, in the clouds, in the face of our children." Reporter Barbara Hey observed that these are "comforting words in a place and time when seeking happiness is often relegated to a 'to-do' list." She then summarized the message: We should feel "a connection to the Earth, engaging and nourishing what is best in all of us and opting not to flame the fires of qualities that harm ourselves and others." Beware of journalistic poets.

Journalistic skeptics who scorn Christian revivalists have become weak in the knees when writing about visiting Buddhist biggies. Teresa Watanabe of the *Los Angeles Times*, beneath an "Insights for Troubled Youths Complete Dalai Lama's Visit" headline, reported how two people came together: "She's just 17, but her world swirls with violence.

. . . He's 64. He's won the Nobel Peace Prize, is regarded as the manifestation of the Buddha of Compassion."

Ms. Watanabe reported seventeen-year-old Monisha gushing, "What he told her will stay with her forever. . . . 'He told me to find self-confidence in my heart and myself. I had tears in my eyes. My heart was beating, like, wild.'" There was more: "'You are your own light,' he told the teenagers. 'Look into your own self.' Some smiled and nodded. Others confessed the teaching went over their heads. But there was no mistaking the impact on them of the day's events." The *Times* did not list the signs of impact or interview "the troubled youths" a year later to see if they had stayed out of trouble, to see if the impact had lasted long enough to keep them out of trouble.

Controversy is a key element of most stories, but reporters allowed none to touch the Dalai Lama. Criticizing Christian anthropology, several newspapers quoted the Dalai Lama saying, "Some people get the impression that we human beings have basically a negative nature. . . . If basic human nature is negative, then there is no future." Christians believe basic human nature is negative, but they still posit a bright future. A back-and-forth here could have edified readers about the differences between the religions, but none was forthcoming.

Syncretism was evident in a *Denver Post* vignette that had a child saying to a monk, "I'm Christian. How can I practice Buddhism?" The response: "If you practice Buddhism, you will become a better Christian." The story embraced cafeteria-style theology—combine something from religion

A with other elements of religions B and C—and quoted the monk explaining, "'If you are committed to eating oranges, it does not prevent you from having a kiwi or a mango, and still eating oranges.'"

The *Houston Chronicle* reported on a Buddhist temple with good things to say about Christ: "In Buddhism, we believe that Jesus Christ is one of the Buddhas," said John Lin, chairman of the temple's board. "He came to this world to help other people." The *Austin American-Statesman* similarly promoted a program in which Christians were said to be "using Buddhist meditation to find a calm that they say brings them closer to God."

Many stories ascribed as special to Buddhism some goals and practices shared by other religions. Seattle readers could learn that Buddhism helps people "change the way in which they think about the world, themselves, and others" and that Buddhists "recognize the things over which they have influence, while also learning to let go of the things they can't control." They could learn "that Buddhism is a matter of transforming minds, which can then transform experience."

The *Dallas Morning News* quoted a new Buddhist, Tifany Henderson, who was promoting Buddhism because "we could all use more peace and less stress." According to the *Los Angeles Times,* the Buddhist goal is "to take life's ups and downs in a balanced and centered way." The *Deseret News* noted that Buddhists teach "correct posture" and provide "guiding principles" such as honesty, openness, love, and compassion that help us develop "an appropriate response to any given situation." Perhaps one signal of journalists' nonattachment to Christianity is the claim of some that these principles are Buddhist.

A typical piece about Buddhism in the *Seattle Times* noted that city resident George Draffan, after his father and others close to him died, "reacted to these personal crises by searching for some sort of spiritual support or belief system that could help him cope. His search led him to Buddhism, of which he said, 'I think the thing that attracts a lot of Westerners is stress. . . . If you get into [Buddhism], you can't do without it. It's a much more productive way of dealing with problems than drinking beer.'" The article publicized an upcoming Buddhist festival "which organizers say could draw up to several hundred people, is open to the public and will feature music, food, dance, meditation, chanting, informational tables, and presentations."

Maybe with such free publicity, more than several hundred would show up, but would anyone ask hard questions? One Buddhist speaker in Dallas said that people must honor "all other beings, including humans, animals, and even the smallest insect. 'We are all equally the same,' he said, referring to humans and all creatures, big and small." The reporter did not point out that behind that democratic notion, which suggests the happy idea that people should be kind to dogs and deer, lies an equation of humans with cockroaches.

Coverage of Islam

Many newspapers and magazines offered crash courses in the basics of Islam following the destruction of the

World Trade Center towers; but those basics were almost always presented in stories that advocated the positive, toleration, without coming to grips with the negative, the existence for centuries of a sizable war party within Islam. Instead of describing both faces of Islam, reporters displayed superficiality and tried to foster syncretism.

Superficiality was evident in reporters' frequent labeling of Osama bin Laden's pronouncements as deviations from moralistic but peace-loving Islam. For example, the *Riverside* (Calif.) *Press-Enterprise* contrasted "self-declared 'Islamic militants'" with the "authentic Islam" absorbed by convert Nancy Hadiza Collins: "'I used to love drinking strawberry margaritas,' she said. 'Now I read Muslim books and avoid sleazy films or music.'"

On the other side of the United States, the *Orlando Sentinel* told readers that "Muslims Strive to Educate," which means that "when Errol Peterkin says Islam is peace, it's more than just an expression. 'It's how we live, by nature of our religion.'" The *Sentinel* reported that at an open house for the Muslim Academy of Central Florida "kindergartners did finger paintings, some students created collages, and older children wrote essays. 'The terrorists called themselves Muslim, but Muslims do not behave with such violence and evil,' wrote fifth-grader Sufeya Yasin."

Reporters suggested that such prepubescent wisdom should just about end the discussion. The *Atlanta Journal* was typical in its statement that discussions in Muslim countries are open-ended: "Most Americans probably would be stunned to see that the Quran advises Muslims to 'be

215

courteous when you argue with People of the Book [Christians and Jews], except with those who do evil.'" The *Journal* did not mention that many Muslims view Christian evangelism as evil. Instead, readers were told, "Although Islam is often depicted in Western thought and popular culture as 'a religion of the sword,' the Quran condemns war and violence."

Sadly the U.S. press had not delved into the debate about what kind of war and violence the Quran condemns. Let's look at several Arabic words. Saddam Hussein and Saudi members of the Wahhabi sect called terrorists martyrs: They paid $25,000 or more to the surviving families of mujahideen (holy warriors) who participate in jihad and become *shahidin* (martyrs). But other Muslims call terrorists *mufsidoon* (evildoers) engaged in *hirabah* (unholy war against society) and heading not to paradise but to *jahannam* (eternal hellfire).

Muslims originally used the term *hirabah* to condemn vicious attacks by members of barbarian tribes who murdered or enslaved those they fought and defeated. Such barbarians engaged in "war against society," often attacking, as do today's terrorists, without discriminating between soldiers and civilians. The TrueSpeak Institute in Washington argues that traditional Islamic law bans "the fomenting of hatred between communities, religions, nations and civilizations; committing and enticing others to commit suicide for the purpose of intimidation; and wanton killing of innocents and noncombatants, even including fellow Muslims."

The question of definition—jihad or hirabah—is crucial for Muslims, but most Americans are unaware of the debate. A Lexis-Nexis search early in 2003 showed seven references to hirabah in the previous ninety days and thousands to jihad. That debate is on among Islamic scholars, though. For example, Ezzeddin Ibrahim of the United Arab Emirates stated that "what occurred on Sept. 11, 2001, is one of the most loathsome of crimes, which in Islam goes under the name of al-hirabah."

Similarly, Akbar Ahmed, chairman of Islamic Studies at American University, said that "al-Qaeda's brand of suicide mass murder and its fomenting of hatred among races, religions, and cultures do not constitute godly or holy jihad—but, in fact, constitute the heinous crime and sin of unholy hirabah." Tamman Adi, director of the Islamic Cultural Center in Eugene, Oregon, also argued that "the masterminds of international terrorism are not fighting a jihad, they are hirabah thugs."

These and other assertions can be found on Internet sites but not in U.S. newspapers, according to my Lexis-Nexis search. Some Americans think Islam is a religion of war and others a religion of peace, but few see that it is and has been both at various times, and that a furious debate concerning Islam's future direction is now under way.

Stories about Islam regularly showed syncretism as well. Conversion from any religion to another is a major step, yet reporters—apparently coming from the view that Islam and Christianity are essentially similar religions—have generally made it seem easy. The *Houston Chronicle,* under a "Drawn to

Islam" headline, concentrated on food, not faith: "Huevos rancheros for breakfast; fasouliye for dinner. . . . For El-Kassir, a Mexican-American convert to Islam, starting the day with the Mexican egg breakfast and ending it with a Lebanese meat-and-bean dinner meant nothing more than the merging of cultures easily found in Islam." Nothing more than the merging of cultures?

Syncretism was also evident in a *Dallas Morning News* report (also under the headline, "Drawn to Islam") on an army officer sent in 1992 to Pakistan, where "the piety of the people made a strong impression. 'They were good, humble people trying to practice their religion,' he said, [so he was] attracted by Islam's strict moral code, a belief system with similarities to Judaism and Christianity." Islam's minutely detailed moral code is different from Christianity's emphasis on broad principles that require discerning application.

Some stories on Muslim holidays did report customs that would seem strange to many Americans but almost always without any explanation of what the differences signify. For example, *The Ledger* (Lakeland, Fla.) reported the celebration of Eid al-Adha, Islam's three-day festival of sacrifice, and noted, "The sacrifice and cooking of a goat or other animal is part of the ritual of the Eid al-Adha. . . . In the Islamic holy book, the Quran, Abraham is said to have been commanded by God to sacrifice his son, Ishmael, but was stopped at the last moment and given a goat to sacrifice instead." *The Ledger* did not explain that sacrifices came because of the under-standing that sin had to be paid for in some manner.

Major theological differences tended to be reported in an "oh, by the way" manner: In Jacksonville, the *Florida Times-Union* stated that "Muslims believe in all of God's prophets, including Jesus Christ. However, they believe Muhammad was the last and final prophet." Oh, that's it? But Christianity is based on the belief not that Christ is one among many prophets but that he is the Son of God. Many newspapers have reported variations on this theme: "Same God: Muslims accept the teachings of the Jewish Torah and the Christian Gospels." That's not true; Muslims accept those teachings only when they conform to the teachings of the Quran, and often they do not.

Chapter Ten
How to Do Better

Ever since *Time* a generation ago ran its famous "Is God Dead?" cover, many journalists have awaited the funeral. Few have altered their expectations as evidence of continued life has poured in. General attitudes among the New York and Washington reporters I know remind me of the story of an elderly man who lay dying in his bed. He suddenly smelled the aroma of his favorite chocolate chip cookies wafting up the stairs. He gathered his remaining strength, forced himself down the stairs, and gazed into the kitchen. Spread out upon platters on the kitchen table were literally hundreds of his favorite chocolate chip cookies. Mustering one great final effort, he threw himself toward the table. He reached out, but—smack!—a spatula came down on his hand. "Stay out of those," his wife growled. "They're for the funeral."

Across the country America's daily newspapers can report the funeral but are ill-equipped to report and understand the new vibrancy of twenty-first-century American religion. That's because they invest little in religion reporting generally, and the reporters they do hire (often one religion reporter per major newspaper) tend to reflect the left-of-center ideologies of the newsrooms in which they serve. Although the Religion Newswriters Association does not report members' affiliations, and many journalists will not explicitly disclose their own beliefs, characteristic story framing suggests rampant theological liberalism.

For example, even in reporting a numbers story of denominational rise and fall, RNA President Sandi Dolbee (*San Diego Union*) evidenced a liberal bias by using as her expert, and quoting uncritically, the Rev. Emma Moore-Kochlacs, a United Methodist superintendent. She attributed conservative growth to stylistic issues and an unwillingness to grapple with hard questions. "'For the most part evangelical churches are more informal in style,'" Moore-Kochlacs said. "In addition, many people are attracted to conservative churches because they are looking for black-and-white theological answers" instead of more complex and realistic "answers to their life questions in the context of religious beliefs."

Dolbee did not say, or have anyone saying, that conservative churches are growing because people want to take the Bible seriously: those who believe it to be God's message logically try to live their lives by it. That understanding is evidently foreign to Michael Paulson, religion writer of the *Boston Globe*. Whether he is covering Christian, Jewish, Muslim, Hindu, or Buddhist groups, he almost never quotes or even refers to the scriptures of those religions. Queried about that by one of my students, Paulson responded that "my main focus is on coverage of contemporary news events and trends (lived religion), so my work is less reliant on those sources than is academic research."

Uh-huh. But what about reporting a conflict within the Presbyterian Church (USA) over ordaining gay elders? The PCUSA *Book of Order* states, "The church confesses the Scriptures to be the Word of God." Isn't it relevant to ask, then, how the denomination interprets verses such as Leviticus 18:22 in the Old Testament ("You shall not lie with a male as with a woman. It is an abomination" NKJV) and equivalent condemnations in the New, such as that in Romans 1:26–27? By largely omitting discussion of the Bible in his reporting, Paulson moved the debate from whether the Bible is from God and how to interpret it to an essentially political argument over gay rights.

Four hundred miles to the south, *Washington Post* religion reporter Hanna Rosin was one of the few journalists to offer any criticism of the Dalai Lama. She wrote that he "spoon-feeds his audience a kind of fortune-cookie Buddhism" and noted the difficulty of maintaining a critical temperament: "It's hard to hold his mushiness against him, given how genial the Dalai Lama is in person." But Rosin did not give such a break to Christians opposed to homosexuality. For example, under a headline "Gay Activists Interrupt Catholic Bishops' Conference," Rosin wrote that the activists' goal was to "remind bishops that 'the official teachings of the Roman Catholic Church about sexual minorities lead to suffering and death.'" Rosin's skilled word choice, "remind," subtly indicated that the bishops *forgot* or *should have already known* the supposed deadly impact of their official position against homosexuality. In other words, the bishops were hypocritically neglecting their own teaching.

The story's lead paragraph reported "a demonstration by a small group of activists who attempted to take communion at a Mass attended by 300 bishops but were refused. Seven protesters from the group 'Rainbow Sash' were denied the Eucharist at an evening Mass at the National Shrine of the Immaculate Conception." A newspaper like the *Washington Post* every day ignores dozens of protests carried out by far more than seven people. But in this case it not only played up the seven but even one: "Janice Sevre-Duszynska of the Women's Ordination Conference seized the microphone and asked the conference room packed with bishops to address the wrong done to 'women called by God to ordination.' The Catholic Church does not ordain women as priests."

The Rosin article showed the role of major newspapers in *certification*: sympathetic journalists can magnify hugely the influence of only seven persons (or even just one) by proclaiming their issues as important, their goals as meritorious, and their actions as courageous. Newspaper coverage can also disparage; for example, Yonat Shimron, the religion reporter of the (Raleigh) *News and Observer* and an RNA officer, provided a cartoon version of strict constructionist beliefs: "Many people who pick up the Bible assume it contains a neat and tidy transcript of the complete word of God as dictated to a set of eager scribes."

Go deeper into the Bible Belt, to a small city like Lakeland, Florida, and theological liberalism persists. Cary McMullen, religion editor for the Lakeland *Ledger* since fall

2000, is an ordained minister in the liberal Presbyterian Church USA and holds postgraduate degrees in religion and divinity from Duke University and Duke Divinity School. That background shows when he dealt with gay and feminist issues, as in "Reform Rabbi Weighs United Same-Sex Couples in Polk" and "Lakeside Baptist Has Woman Minister." In both stories he quoted only sources supporting homosexual unions and female pastors. McMullen also tended to hype rather than probe eastern religions; one article, "Buddhists Bloom in Jail Ministry," included a positively contextualized quotation, "Grace is just having to deal with one thing," and did not explain from whom the grace is purportedly coming within a religion that does not recognize a personal God.

Down the coast in Palm Beach, Steve Gushee, a religion reporter for five years who is now a columnist, frankly wrote to one of my students about his agenda: "I am driven to write about religion because it is the most powerful force on earth. . . . Most of the world's danger points are rooted in religion on some profound level . . . India/Pakistan, Northern Ireland, Palestine/Israel, the Catholics, Orthodox and Muslims of the Balkans, the influence of the religious right in this country and on and on." Gushee wrote that to promote peace "the official teaching of religious groups needs to repudiate all claims to exclusive truth and genuinely welcome the insights of other faiths as effective means of full union with God."

Gushee has been particularly hard on Christian conservatives. For example, he argued in October 2002, that "Jerry Falwell is not the buffoon many people think he is. He is an effective preacher of dangerous and distorted ideas, [preaching] a skewed vision of the Christian faith that is rooted in judgment and nourished by fear and the exclusion of others. This is in sharp contrast to the normative Christian faith that is rooted in forgiveness and nurtured by love and acceptance. . . . [His] faith convictions come from the same scary theology that fuels the Ku Klux Klan, Oklahoma bomber Timothy McVeigh and the Muslims of Al-Qaeda, who distort Islam in much the same way."

Move across the country to Riverside, California, and the work of Hieu Tran Pham, religion reporter for the *Press-Enterprise* in Riverside, California, a 200,000-circulation newspaper, comes into focus. He told one of my students, "Being an agnostic helps immensely in my efforts to remain balanced as a journalist." His lack of belief has kept him from siding with any one religion, but the belief that no religion contains the truth leads him to suggest in stories that tolerance is the paramount virtue.

To serve the cause of tolerance, Pham has consistently accentuated the positives of Islam and buried concern about the negatives. A profile of Mohammad M. Hossain, a doctor who ran clinics in Redlands and Riverside, emphasized how his family was skipping television during Ramadan: "They have mapped out a full schedule of scripture study, house decorating and get-togethers for neighbors and coworkers. . . . Mautasim, 9, chimed in: 'It's easier to forget TV 'cause we have lots of other fun stuff.' Right about now, the kids are helping their parents put up a large, plastic banner that reads, 'Happy Ramadan!'" Three weeks later, a story about three men who have each memorized the Quran explained how one "deepened his faith in social diversity by analyzing the Quran from start to finish." That's all very well, but it would be useful to readers to learn what a careful analysis of the Quran's teaching about violence reveals.

The same tilt is evident in the work of Teresa Watanabe, the *Los Angeles Times'* head religion reporter. Watanabe's great-grandfather was one of the first Japanese men to graduate from Yale Divinity School and be ordained as a minister. Later he returned to Japan, reembraced Buddhism, tried to syncretize the two religions, and had two funerals, one Christian and one Buddhist. Watanabe's parents, one a Catholic and the other an agnostic, exposed her and her seven siblings to many religious traditions, and the reporter told one of my students that she embraces all religious paths and is "gravitating toward an impulse of reconciliation" that makes her more likely to cover "a Muslim-Jewish dialogue group than an anti-Islam or anti-Jewish group." She and her husband attend both a Catholic church and a Buddhist temple.

Reconciliation is all to the good, but Watanabe's previous experience (she had been the *Times'* Tokyo bureau chief) certainly showed her that opposing views can sometimes not be reconciled. Watanabe has written several articles that go beyond stereotypes, but she generally has avoided controversy and acknowledges a penchant for writing positive stories that seem fluffy. She, like many other religion reporters, is particularly affectionate toward feminists pressing for the ordination of women.

Watanabe even traveled to Erie, Pennsylvania (clearly a location that is not obligatory for a Los Angeles reporter to cover), so as to report on "The Nuns Who Defied Vatican's Order to Be Silent." That story described residents of a monastic community who lived "in the wooded meadows off Lake Erie . . . . They sing the Psalms. They feed the poor, train the illiterate." But Eden did not last: "The gentle rhythms of their ancient religious lifestyle recently exploded in a radical act of conscience. . . . Sister Joan Chittister, a renowned feminist, [continued to lecture about] feminist spirituality. She warns that society will collapse without a balance to what she calls the patriarchal values of superiority, dominance, effectiveness and conformity." Chittister received support from other nuns in her battle: "Gag order or no, Chittister intends to keep talking. It took 400 years of debate to end church support for slavery, she notes." Using loaded language such as "gag order"—the sentence could have been, "Breaking her vows or not"—Watanabe and other journalists equated their antipatriarchy drive with antislavery campaigns.

On the other hand, Watanabe's nonmaterialist background does lead her toward sympathy for those who suggest that intelligent design rather than random chance underlies the development of the universe and life itself. She wrote in 2001 about how "a high school biology teacher named Roger DeHart set out to question Darwin's theories of evolution. He never mentioned God. He dissected such scientific topics as bacterial flagella, fossil records and embryonic development. Examine the evidence, he told the students, and ponder the Big Question: Is life the result of random, meaningless events? Or was it designed by an intelligent force?"

That's a more balanced presentation than such questioning normally receives. Watanabe continued, "Over nine years, DeHart would introduce ideas about this theory of 'intelligent design.' Then a student protested that DeHart was pushing religion. Then the ACLU filed a complaint. In 1999, school authorities ordered DeHart to drop references to design and stick to the textbook. Last week, DeHart was told he could not even introduce materials questioning Darwin's theories." Watanabe was portraying DeHart not as a rube but as the victim of censorship.

Watanabe also noted that the intelligent design movement has more "intellectual firepower, mainstream appeal and academic respectability" than earlier critics of Darwinism. She offered a fair summary of the importance of the debate: "Design advocates aim to reshape modern intellectual culture by marshaling scientific evidence that life was created by a transcendent mind, rather than by impersonal, random natural forces." So it's not as if religion reporting is all tilted, or that there's no way to do better.

In a book solely devoted to religion reporting, we could further explore beliefs of religion reporters—they may differ from the attitudes of reporters generally—but the crucial object for analysis is not so much journalistic attitude as journalistic production. Some defenders of the modern reportorial faith have argued that journalists can keep their biases to themselves and complete the extraordinary task of writing no-spin articles that can retain reader interest. I've argued against that notion in books such as *Prodigal Press* and *Telling the Truth*, and my students and I found that religion coverage in U.S. newspapers tends to fall into three categories.

Almost all stories about Buddhism, Hinduism, and Judaism are what we called *type one* articles: public relations for the religion, a presentation of the sunny side often emphasizing customs and ceremonies. Most stories about Islam also accentuate the positive, often as a counterpoint to animosity readers might feel because of terrorism. Some of the stories on Islam (and even more on Christianity) could be called *type two* stories that go beyond public relations to critiques of a religion based on today's politically correct analysis. A level two story, for example, might criticize the treatment of women in Islam or the attitude toward homosexuality among Christians. The truly rare stories are *type three,* going beyond happy talk or conventional analysis to a depiction of how the downsides of some religions may be imbedded in their positives. For example, Buddhism gets a great press for its antimaterialism, but journalists should show how Buddhists are to practice nonattachment not only to things but to people as well.

Another way of charting story slants is by seeing what journalists praise as the highest level of spiritual development. Traditionally theists have argued that faith in God logically requires assent to the proposition that God is wiser than us. Long ago Augustine said, "If you believe in the gospel that you like, and reject what you don't like, it is not the gospel you believe, but yourself." That understanding came under challenge in the twentieth century. Lawrence

Kohlberg, for example, became known for proclaiming ethical stages through which he thought people should move from following the law to "social duty" and perhaps to "autonomous ethical thinking," wherein a person makes up his own principles. I'd suggest that in this highest stage humans are the most selfish, virtually inventing a world totally apart from God, but Kohlberg saw such ethical autonomy as the goal of human existence.

Many journalism students and journalists I've talked with over the past several years express faith in their own autonomous judgment. One typical reporter said, "I make my decisions based on what I feel is right." Another said he affirmed some Christian principles, but "the bottom line is I believe in me." A third said, "My governing belief is the only person you can really trust in life is yourself." A fourth believed in "taking bits of pieces from several religions and in that way making up my own, personal religion."

Religion reporters have tended to praise (as the *Washington Post* did in 2001) those who "write their own Bible. They fashion their own God . . . turning him into a social planner, therapist or guardian angel." The *Post* told the story of Ed and Joanne Liverani, who decided to "build their own church, salvaging bits of their old religion they liked and chucking the rest." They ended up with a god who "cheers them up when they're sad, laughs at their quirks." Lynn Garrett, a religious book tracker for *Publishers Weekly,* called this "an eclectic approach. People borrow ideas from different traditions, then add them to whatever religion they're used to."

Since that philosophy underlies many story perspectives, it's harder to find examples of accurate and thoughtful articles than of those exuding superficiality and syncretism, but a few do pop up. The *Los Angeles Times* ran a profile of Hindu villagers who "depend almost entirely on the coins and bowls of wheat flour they receive as alms. It has been this way for at least a century because, the villagers say, they have been born to honor the Hindu god Krishna with song and outstretched hands . . . the beggars of Ranidongri say they are simply following in sacred footsteps." The *Times* quoted villager Sadaram Mukutwansi, thirty-two, saying, "I blame my own karma. If god didn't give me poverty, then we wouldn't have [to beg] in the first place." The key is karma: Begging "is punishment for being just as mean to other beggars in a previous life, Mukutwansi believes."

The article described how "in the beggars' village, Mukutwansi squatted on a plastic mat sewn from pieces of old sacks. . . . He takes his only son, Lokeshi, 10, with him to beg in a group of about a dozen people, who travel by train—if they can beg a free spot on the floor—to reach the several cities where they sing for handouts. Most days, his alms amount to about 45 cents and a little flour." Bad karma forces Mukutwansi to beg and also to consume "the local brew, moonshine made from the flowers of the mahua tree, which produces a liquid said to be potent enough to keep a motorcycle running in an emergency." Villagers "go out to beg for five to six months," then "come back and mostly spend [alms] on drinking."

The *Washington Post* presented another pathetic outcome of religious misunderstanding when in 2001 it reported on Nepal's crown prince killing nine other members of the royal family (including his parents) and then himself. According to "the prevailing worldview in Nepal, based on Hindu teachings," the incident occurred because "the members of the royal family brought only short lives into their most recent incarnations based on actions in previous existences." Mukunda Raj Aryal, fifty-eight, a professor and Brahman, added that the crown prince should be honored for having "acted well the villainous part he was assigned" by karma.

Two other U.S. newspapers gave a sense of the difference between Hinduism's high theology and common practice. The *New York Times,* under a headline "Braving Nature and Militants, Hindus Trek for a Peek at a God's Icy Symbol," reported from Kashmir about a cult object: "Barefoot, world-renouncing Hindu monks, naked to the waist and wrapped in orange cloth below, came walking, carrying tridents. . . . Over a month, more than 100,000 Hindu pilgrims will hike at least 19 miles, sleep in freezing temperatures above 10,000 feet and brave attacks from Muslim militants. Their trek is all for a hurried glimpse of an ice stalagmite that forms each year on a wall of a remote cave here. The nine-foot-tall ice sheet, shaped like a phallus, is considered to be the symbol of Lord Shiva, one of Hinduism's three most revered gods."

The outcome wasn't all that Hindu visitors hoped for: "After crossing a small snowfield, arriving pilgrims took a ritual bath in a pristine stream and put on fresh clothes. They then waited for two hours in a long line that snaked up a set

of stairs leading to the cave. Hailing Shiva and ringing ceremonial bells, they took a final few steps, pressed themselves
against an iron railing and looked at the cave wall. The towering, nine-foot ice form had apparently melted. It was only
one foot tall. Some pilgrims, it must be said, were disap-
pointed with the size. Others lamented that they were forced
to leave after only seconds, saying the police had pulled them
away before they could confess sins and make requests of
Lord Shiva."

The *Chicago Sun-Times* under a headline, "4,000 on Hand
for Monkey's Funeral," offered a story from New Delhi about
how "4,000 devotees attended the funeral in southern India
Sunday of a monkey they believed to be the incarnation of
a Hindu god. The animal strayed several weeks ago into
a temple dedicated to the monkey god Hanuman in
Timmaganipalli village. Villagers refused to release it, and
hundreds visited the monkey each day, seeking its blessing
and garlanding it with flowers."

The story did not have a happy ending: "Animal-rights
activists said the monkey, which collapsed on Saturday, died
of starvation and exhaustion. When the villagers discovered
the monkey sitting on Hanuman's idol, they thought it was
a reincarnation of the ancient god and refused to let it out of
the temple. . . . India is dotted with tens of thousands
of Hanuman temples, and every Tuesday is reserved for his
worship. Anyone trying to catch monkeys, however destructive they may be, is beaten or chased away."

That same sense of the bizarre is not apparent in coverage of Hinduism within the United States—yet the same

theology underlies Hindu worship inside and outside India. Coverage of Buddhism is similar: the overwhelming majority of stories about Buddhism were superficial and syncretistic, and the two articles from U.S. publications that went beyond public relations concerned Buddhism abroad.

First, Uwe Siemon-Netto of United Press International (under the headline "Buddhism's Pedophile Monks") showed the dark side of some Buddhist practices: "Sex between clergymen and boys is by no means a uniquely Catholic phenomenon, a noted American scholar said Wednesday— it's been going on in Buddhist monasteries in Asia for centuries." University of Wisconsin Professor Leonard Zwilling told Siemon-Netto, "Of course, this is against the Buddhist canon, but it has been common in Tibet, China, Japan, and elsewhere. In fact, when the Jesuits arrived in China and Japan in the 16th century, they were horrified by the formalized relationships between Buddhist monks and novices who were still children. These relationships clearly broke the celibacy rule."

Buddhist pedophilia has a long background and is still a concern, Siemon-Netto reported: "Some 2,500 years ago, the outrageous behavior of one pandaka (homosexual, in Pali, the sacred language of Theravada Buddhism) prompted the Buddha to ban the ordination of such men." UPI included Mr. Zwilling's citation of twentieth-century "incidents where members of the Bob-Dob, an order enforcing discipline among Tibetan monks, fought each other over boys."

Second, Joshua Kurlantzick in *The New Republic* wrote that his view of Buddhism "was shaped by the American media, which usually portrays Buddhists as pure, serene, and incorruptible." But then he attended a Buddhist seminar in Bangkok and spoke with Thais who told him of "saffron-robed Buddhist monks guilty of graft, lechery, and other crimes." Mr. Kurlantzick first "chuckled skeptically at their tales" but then found that the stories of rape, orgiastic sex, and murder were true and "especially shocking because so many Westerners assume Buddhism to be fundamentally different from other faiths. It isn't. . . . Not that any of this is undermining Buddhism's reputation in the West. . . . American disciples won't let reality get in the way of their preconceptions about the religion."

Some newspapers in Australia also were willing to fight Buddhist public relations. Under the headline "Buddha in Suburbia," Joyce Morgan of the *Sydney Morning Herald* asked whether Buddhism is "a temporary staging post for aging baby boomers." Disillusionment with materialism is key to the appeal of Buddhism, which teaches that "the solutions lie within ourselves." That's a welcome notion to boomers who don't want to be part of "Christianity, with its emphasis on God the Father [that] evokes a parent-child bond. In short, a vertical relationship."

Morgan traced the history:

> One of the biggest influences on the spread of Buddhism in the West was the emergence of the hippie trail through India and Nepal in the 1960s and 1970s. Some of these psychedelic dreamers

were no doubt muddle-headed as they clutched
their books by Lobsang Rampa, the so-called mystic monk who turned out to be Cyril Hoskins,
a British clerk. . . . Not that the Tibetans were
enamored of the dope-smoking Westerners filling
their rucksacks with prayer beads and incense. . . .
The hippies were viewed with suspicion as
people who had run out of things to do in the
world and were looking for novelty. And perhaps
they were. . . . Buddhism may appear fashionable
today and some will no doubt discard it with last
season's flares.

The Age (Melbourne) also came through with a profile of
one woman who became intensely Buddhist after her partner
committed suicide: "You ask me what brought me to
Buddhism?" Jenny Kee says. "Suffering. Suffering and great
pain." Others, however, dabble: "Many more people profess
vague allegiance to the ideals of Buddhism than are card-
carrying members. . . . Buddhism in the West does not ask
followers to make a lifelong and exclusive commitment, or to
join a community of believers," and that works well in a culture where people believe "spirituality" but not religion is
important. The article, headlined "Devotees and Dabblers,"
quoted a religion professor's argument that many use
Buddhism in the pursuit of "power, personal autonomy, and
profit." Writer Sophie Cunningham concluded, "Precisely
because it is so easy-going, Buddhism can be seen as just
another New Age philosophy."

Shefalee Vasudev of *India Today* set a particularly colorful article, "New Buddhism: The Buddha Bar," on "the eve of the 67th birthday of His Holiness, the Dalai Lama. Up in the hills of Himachal Pradesh in the small town of Mcleodganj near Dharamsala, some students of Buddhist philosophy sway in abandon to the beats of a techno-trance number that plays loudly at a rave party . . . amidst uninhibited smooching, petty arguments, umpteen puffs and sniffs of drugs, the night lingers on."

Mr. Vasudev described "the many groups of beaded, bearded, funkily accessorized moksha-seeking tourists clad in tattered blue jeans with pierced lips and eyebrows who are redefining this religion. . . . They seem to be showing the world that worldly detachment can be on friendly terms with the trappings of desire." He quoted "Gintaras, a Lithuanian who studies Buddhist philosophy, saying, 'This taste of Buddhism is doing me a lot of good since my disillusionment with Christianity turned me into an atheist. Spirituality works only if it is flexible. And unlike most other religions, I find Buddhism open to interpretation. I had thought of experimenting with different concepts, but Hinduism and Islam are not my cup of tea.'"

Mr. Vasudev then quoted "Ideno, a 21-year-old Israeli girl" saying over cups of Tibetan herbal tea, "Peace does not necessarily have to be about passivity. Even as I seek peace, I do not want to withdraw from the path of desire because it will only make me agitated." Sacha Faller, a psychology student from Switzerland, added, "What better way to understand detachment than to have it constantly tested by an indulgent life?" He added, "I had the most intense relationship of my life here, which lasted only 11 days," but lessons in detachment helped him recover.

"The monks too seem to be wading in doubtful waters," Mr. Vasudev concluded. "There is no mistaking the body language of young monks who are seen with girls in restaurants and other public places. Is this an indication that the liberated, neo-Buddhists who crowd the philosophy classes are becoming role models for the monks instead of it being the other way round?"

On Islam, UPI's Siemon-Netto succinctly noted the error of simply saying that both Islam and Christianity "revere Jesus, affirm His virgin birth, and await His ultimate return to judge the living and the dead. Of course there is a huge difference. To Muslims, Jesus is the second-ranking prophet who never died on the cross. To Christians, He is the incarnation of the very aspect of God that created the universe. In Christ, God made Himself small for humanity's salvation. These differences are insuperable, if you wish to engage in an honest theological discourse."

Teresa Watanabe of the *Los Angeles Times* showed what could be done in a detailed piece of reporting (appropriately headlined, "Inside a Complex Community"). The article began, "No place in Southern California symbolizes the tension over Saudi Arabia's influence in the world like the King Fahd Mosque in Culver City. . . . The mosque's leaders admire Muhammad ibn 'Abd al-Wahhab, an 18th-century evangelist. Al-Wahhab inspired the so-called Wahhabi movement, which is prominent in Saudi Arabia but criticized by detractors for oppressing women, shunning non-Muslims, and inspiring Osama bin Laden's jihad."

The article showed how militant and peaceful factions in America's second-largest city are fighting for dominance within a mosque financed by Saudi money: "Inside the mosque community, there are those who are sympathetic to jihad and suicide bombings and those who are not. Some object to non-Muslims visiting their sacred space; others warmly embrace them. Some women veil their entire bodies; others throw off such practices as outdated. . . . On the Friday after the terrorist attacks, the imam [Tajuddin Shuaib] says, he gave a sermon condemning suicide bombings and was shouted down by some men who leaped to their feet and accused him of 'changing the Quran.'"

Watanabe continued, "Patriotic banners supporting President Bush and the families of terrorist victims were torn down from the mosque and stolen, he says. The same hot-heads, Shuaib says, have also tried to foment hatred against Israel for its actions against Palestinians and the United States for its bombing campaign against Afghanistan. . . . Shuaib says he kicked out four members of the mosque in October in part because they were fomenting dissent and extremism."

The article described a kicked-out member, "Abdo Ghanem, 39 . . . a designer-clothes salesman [who] praises America's political freedoms even as he castigates its moral decadence." Mr. Ghanem chauffeured Sheik Omar Abdel Rahman (given life imprisonment for conspiring to blow up New York landmarks) and favors assassination of bad

Muslims and jihad against Saudi Arabia and Israel. But Watanabe also described "Sonia Arcangeli, 31. The Marina del Rey resident paints her nails red, views gender segregation as unequal and, to the horror of other women, dissents from the majority view that menstruating women must not touch the Quran."

Watanabe showed her sympathy for Imam Shuaib, who suffered criticism for performing a wedding that non-Muslim women attended without wearing "proper" covering, and took more heat for accepting flowers from a Jewish neighbor after news broke that the Jewish Defense League allegedly planned to bomb the mosque. "Brother, are you out of your mind?" Shuaib says he told the critic. "Do you want a bomb or flowers? People with extremist views want you to come down very, very hard on non-Muslims."

Sadly, Watanabe's article was unusual, as most reporters implied that Muslim extremists were a small minority. The UPI's Uwe Siemon-Netto was one of few to ask hard questions and still offer hope, in a UPI article provocatively headlined, "Can Islam Be Reformed?" He reported both questions involving the meaning of jihad and problems in Islamic law that can lead to death by stoning for a woman who reports a rape charge. Then he noted Islam's "teaching that about once every 100 years God sends a messenger to correct not the Quran, but the perspective from which it is to be seen at any given time in history." He reported that "a small but intellectually powerful group of Muslim scholars is endeavoring to correct this perspective for our time. Quietly, they are also engaged in dialogues with Jews and Christians, especially in Europe and the United States."

Those dialogues are needed, but they need to stress telling the truth and not showing "compassion" toward Muslims by refusing to ask hard questions. On October 1, 2002, the London Arabic-language daily *Al-Hayat* printed a letter from M. G. Abu Saber, father of a young Palestinian suicide bomber who wrote, "Four months ago, I lost my eldest son when his friends tempted him, praising the path of death. They persuaded him to blow himself up in one of Israel's cities."

The bereaved father went on to describe how "friends of my eldest son the martyr were starting to wrap themselves like snakes around my other son, not yet 17." They wanted "to direct him to the same path towards which they had guided his brother, so that he would blow himself up too to avenge his brother, claiming 'he had nothing to lose.'"

Mr. Saber continued, "From the blood of the wounded heart of a father who has lost what is most precious to him in the world, I turn to the leaders of the Palestinian factions, and at their head the leaders of Hamas and Islamic Jihad and their sheiks, who use religious rulings and statements to urge more and more of the sons of Palestine to their deaths." He asked, "By what right do these leaders send the young people, even young boys in the flower of their youth, to their deaths? Who gave them religious or any other legitimacy to tempt our children and urge them to their deaths? . . . Has death become the only way to restore the rights and liberate the land? And if this be the case, why doesn't a single one of all the sheiks who compete amongst themselves in issuing fiery religious rulings, send his son?"

It is neither wise nor compassionate to remain uninformed about those fiery religious rulings and whether they have a basis in the Quran. Nor is it wise, when one culture may be threatening another, to settle for the most superficial coverage of that culture's belief, or to assume that both cultures have essentially the same understanding of who God is. So I will close with three suggestions that point to tougher religion reporting, not easier.

First, leaders of all religions should be treated as human beings, not plastic figurines. One *Chicago Sun-Times* profile, Debra Pickett's "I Blew My Monkhood," did it right. She showed how the followers of Ann Arbor resident Nawang Gehlek believe him to be the reincarnation of a major lama, even though he rebelled in the 1960s: "'I smoked a pack and a half of cigarettes a day,' he says, and then with made-for-TV delivery, pauses, adding, 'but I did not inhale.' Also, he drank. And some other stuff. . . . Living in India, through his 20s, he did a good bit of the aforementioned experimenting, mostly with American and European 'seekers' who traded their vices for his abbey-trained wisdom. More significantly—to him—he also had a crisis of faith. He wasn't sure he believed in reincarnation, and particularly not his own."

The story showed how devotees would tell him he did wonderful things in his past life, but he could remember nothing. "He felt he couldn't ask his teachers and was afraid of being rejected by his peers if he put his doubts into words. 'Buddhists accept reincarnation just like we accept hamburger,' he says. 'Imagine an American kid asking their parents about hamburger in the 1940s or 1950s. He'd get beaten up, too.'" Throughout, Pickett showed that she had not become weak-kneed in Gehlek's presence: She described him in the way she might a business or political leader whose route to the top had also had some curves.

Pickett's realism leads to me a second suggestion: U.S. newspapers should cover religious groups as they cover political groups. They should not see stories on religion as community relations fodder, or placate critics by running what in essence are press releases. They should report the debate: when a loose constructionist religious leader makes a statement, they should find a strict constructionist who disagrees with him, and vice versa. They should not soft-soap theological differences between Hindus and Muslims or between Christians and Jews. Columnist Don Feder, observing that most Americans oppose gay marriage but most reporters and editors at major media outlets favor it, argues that when journalists "say an issue is 'divisive,' they mean it divides majority opinion from their opinion." Truly divisive issues litter the theological landscape, and reporters trained to bring out controversy in other areas should not redline it in religion.

My third suggestion is that newspapers should offer more of what since Augustine seventeen centuries ago has been a leading human interest genre: realistic conversion stories. Since I came to Christ out of Judaism twenty-eight years ago, I've been interviewed many times about the process, yet no newspaper reporter has gone beyond the superficial. Lauren

Winner's *Girl Meets God* (2002) realistically describes the process in a way that provides both human interest and theological questioning, and reporters could do the same in shorter forms, but none to my knowledge has. Profiles by discerning reporters could bring out religious issues in dramatic relief. Such writers now are hard to find; maybe in a decade a whole corps will have emerged.